BUSINESS MATH HANDBOOK AND STUDY GUIDE

to accompany

Practical Business Math Procedures

Fifth Edition

Jeffrey Slater

© Richard D. Irwin, a Times Mirror Higher Education
Group, Inc. company, 1991, 1994, and 1997

ISBN 0-256-23874-X

IRWIN

Chicago • Bogotá • Boston • Buenos Aires • Caracas
London • Madrid • Mexico City • Sydney • Toronto

PERIOD	COMPOUND INTEREST	PRESENT VALUE	PRESENT VALUE OF ANNUITY	AMOUNT OF ANNUITY	SINKING FUND
1	1.0050	0.9950	0.9950	1.0000	1.0000
2	1.0100	0.9901	1.9851	2.0050	0.4988
3	1.0151	0.9851	2.9702	3.0150	0.3317
4	1.0202	0.9802	3.9505	4.0301	0.2481
5	1.0253	0.9754	4.9259	5.0503	0.1980
6	1.0304	0.9705	5.8964	6.0755	0.1646
7	1.0355	0.9657	6.8621	7.1059	0.1407
8	1.0407	0.9609	7.8230	8.1414	0.1228
9	1.0459	0.9561	8.7791	9.1821	0.1089
10	1.0511	0.9513	9.7304	10.2280	0.0978
11	1.0564	0.9466	10.6770	11.2792	0.0887
12	1.0617	0.9419	11.6189	12.3356	0.0811
13	1.0670	0.9372	12.5562	13.3973	0.0746
14	1.0723	0.9326	13.4887	14.4643	0.0691
15	1.0777	0.9279	14.4166	15.5365	0.0644
16	1.0831	0.9233	15.3399	16.6142	0.0602
17	1.0885	0.9187	16.2586	17.6973	0.0565
18	1.0939	0.9141	17.1728	18.7858	0.0532
19	1.0994	0.9096	18.0824	19.8797	0.0503
20	1.1049	0.9051	18.9874	20.9791	0.0477
21	1.1104	0.9006	19.8880	22.0840	0.0453
22	1.1160	0.8961	20.7841	23.1945	0.0431
23	1.1216	0.8916	21.6757	24.3104	0.0411
24	1.1272	0.8872	22.5629	25.4320	0.0393
25	1.1328	0.8828	23.4457	26.5591	0.0377
26	1.1385	0.8784	24.3240	27.6919	0.0361
27	1.1442	0.8740	25.1980	28.8304	0.0347
28	1.1499	0.8697	26.0677	29.9746	0.0334
29	1.1556	0.8653	26.9331	31.1245	0.0321
30	1.1614	0.8610	27.7941	32.2801	0.0310
31	1.1672	0.8567	28.6508	33.4414	0.0299
32	1.1730	0.8525	29.5033	34.6087	0.0289
33	1.1789	0.8482	30.3515	35.7817	0.0279
34	1.1848	0.8440	31.1956	36.9606	0.0271
35	1.1907	0.8398	32.0354	38.1454	0.0262
36	1.1967	0.8356	32.8710	39.3361	0.0254
37	1.2027	0.8315	33.7025	40.5328	0.0247
38	1.2087	0.8274	34.5299	41.7355	0.0240
39	1.2147	0.8232	35.3531	42.9441	0.0233
40	1.2208	0.8191	36.1723	44.1589	0.0226
41	1.2269	0.8151	36.9873	45.3797	0.0220
42	1.2330	0.8110	37.7983	46.6066	0.0215
43	1.2392	0.8070	38.6053	47.8396	0.0209
44	1.2454	0.8030	39.4083	49.0788	0.0204
45	1.2516	0.7990	40.2072	50.3242	0.0199
46	1.2579	0.7950	41.0022	51.5759	0.0194
47	1.2642	0.7910	41.7932	52.8337	0.0189
48	1.2705	0.7871	42.5804	54.0979	0.0185
49	1.2768	0.7832	43.3635	55.3684	0.0181
50	1.2832	0.7793	44.1428	56.6452	0.0177

1%

PERIOD	COMPOUND INTEREST	PRESENT VALUE	PRESENT VALUE OF ANNUITY	AMOUNT OF ANNUITY	SINKING FUND
1	1.0100	0.9901	0.9901	1.0000	1.0000
2	1.0201	0.9803	1.9704	2.0100	0.4975
3	1.0303	0.9706	2.9410	3.0301	0.3300
4	1.0406	0.9610	3.9020	4.0604	0.2463
5	1.0510	0.9515	4.8534	5.1010	0.1960
6	1.0615	0.9420	5.7955	6.1520	0.1625
7	1.0721	0.9327	6.7282	7.2135	0.1386
8	1.0829	0.9235	7.6517	8.2857	0.1207
9	1.0937	0.9143	8.5660	9.3685	0.1067
10	1.1046	0.9053	9.4713	10.4622	0.0956
11	1.1157	0.8963	10.3676	11.5668	0.0865
12	1.1268	0.8874	11.2551	12.6825	0.0788
13	1.1381	0.8787	12.1337	13.8093	0.0724
14	1.1495	0.8700	13.0037	14.9474	0.0669
15	1.1610	0.8613	13.8650	16.0969	0.0621
16	1.1726	0.8528	14.7179	17.2579	0.0579
17	1.1843	0.8444	15.5622	18.4304	0.0543
18	1.1961	0.8360	16.3983	19.6147	0.0510
19	1.2081	0.8277	17.2260	20.8109	0.0481
20	1.2202	0.8195	18.0455	22.0190	0.0454
21	1.2324	0.8114	18.8570	23.2392	0.0430
22	1.2447	0.8034	19.6604	24.4716	0.0409
23	1.2572	0.7954	20.4558	25.7163	0.0389
24	1.2697	0.7876	21.2434	26.9735	0.0371
25	1.2824	0.7798	22.0231	28.2432	0.0354
26	1.2953	0.7720	22.7952	29.5256	0.0339
27	1.3082	0.7644	23.5596	30.8209	0.0324
28	1.3213	0.7568	24.3164	32.1291	0.0311
29	1.3345	0.7493	25.0658	33.4504	0.0299
30	1.3478	0.7419	25.8077	34.7849	0.0287
31	1.3613	0.7346	26.5423	36.1327	0.0277
32	1.3749	0.7273	27.2696	37.4941	0.0267
33	1.3887	0.7201	27.9897	38.8690	0.0257
34	1.4026	0.7130	28.7027	40.2577	0.0248
35	1.4166	0.7059	29.4086	41.6603	0.0240
36	1.4308	0.6989	30.1075	43.0769	0.0232
37	1.4451	0.6920	30.7995	44.5076	0.0225
38	1.4595	0.6852	31.4847	45.9527	0.0218
39	1.4741	0.6784	32.1630	47.4122	0.0211
40	1.4889	0.6717	32.8347	48.8864	0.0205
41	1.5038	0.6650	33.4997	50.3752	0.0199
42	1.5188	0.6584	34.1581	51.8790	0.0193
43	1.5340	0.6519	34.8100	53.3978	0.0187
44	1.5493	0.6454	35.4554	54.9317	0.0182
45	1.5648	0.6391	36.0945	56.4811	0.0177
46	1.5805	0.6327	36.7272	58.0459	0.0172
47	1.5963	0.6265	37.3537	59.6263	0.0168
48	1.6122	0.6203	37.9739	61.2226	0.0163
49	1.6283	0.6141	38.5881	62.8348	0.0159
50	1.6446	0.6080	39.1961	64.4632	0.0155

PERIOD	COMPOUND INTEREST	PRESENT VALUE	PRESENT VALUE OF ANNUITY	AMOUNT OF ANNUITY	SINKING FUND
1	1.0150	0.9852	0.9852	1.0000	1.0000
2	1.0302	0.9707	1.9559	2.0150	0.4963
3	1.0457	0.9563	2.9122	3.0452	0.3284
4	1.0614	0.9422	3.8544	4.0909	0.2444
5	1.0773	0.9283	4.7826	5.1522	0.1941
6	1.0934	0.9145	5.6972	6.2295	0.1605
7	1.1098	0.9010	6.5982	7.3230	0.1366
8	1.1265	0.8877	7.4859	8.4328	0.1186
9	1.1434	0.8746	8.3605	9.5593	0.1046
10	1.1605	0.8617	9.2222	10.7027	0.0934
11	1.1780	0.8489	10.0711	11.8632	0.0843
12	1.1960	0.8364	10.9075	13.0412	0.0767
13	1.2135	0.8240	11.7315	14.2368	0.0702
14	1.2318	0.8119	12.5433	15.4503	0.0647
15	1.2502	0.7999	13.3432	16.6821	0.0599
16	1.2690	0.7880	14.1312	17.9323	0.0558
17	1.2880	0.7764	14.9076	19.2013	0.0521
18	1.3073	0.7649	15.6725	20.4893	0.0488
19	1.3270	0.7536	16.4261	21.7966	0.0459
20	1.3469	0.7425	17.1686	23.1236	0.0432
21	1.3671	0.7315	17.9001	24.4704	0.0409
22	1.3876	0.7207	18.6208	25.8375	0.0387
23	1.4084	0.7100	19.3308	27.2250	0.0367
24	1.4295	0.6995	20.0304	28.6334	0.0349
25	1.4510	0.6892	20.7196	30.0629	0.0333
26	1.4727	0.6790	21.3986	31.5138	0.0317
27	1.4948	0.6690	22.0676	32.9866	0.0303
28	1.5172	0.6591	22.7267	34.4813	0.0290
29	1.5400	0.6494	23.3760	35.9986	0.0278
30	1.5631	0.6398	24.0158	37.5385	0.0266
31	1.5865	0.6303	24.6461	39.1016	0.0256
32	1.6103	0.6210	25.2671	40.6881	0.0246
33	1.6345	0.6118	25.8789	42.2984	0.0236
34	1.6590	0.6028	26.4817	43.9329	0.0228
35	1.6839	0.5939	27.0755	45.5919	0.0219
36	1.7091	0.5851	27.6606	47.2758	0.0212
37	1.7348	0.5764	28.2371	48.9849	0.0204
38	1.7608	0.5679	28.8050	50.7197	0.0197
39	1.7872	0.5595	29.3645	52.4805	0.0191
40	1.8140	0.5513	29.9158	54.2677	0.0184
41	1.8412	0.5431	30.4589	56.0817	0.0178
42	1.8688	0.5351	30.9940	57.9229	0.0173
43	1.8969	0.5272	31.5212	59.7917	0.0167
44	1.9253	0.5194	32.0405	61.6886	0.0162
45	1.9542	0.5117	32.5523	63.6139	0.0157
46	1.9835	0.5042	33.0564	65.5681	0.0153
47	2.0133	0.4967	33.5531	67.5516	0.0148
48	2.0435	0.4894	34.0425	69.5649	0.0144
49	2.0741	0.4821	34.5246	71.6084	0.0140
50	2.1052	0.4750	34.9996	73.6825	0.0136

2%

PERIOD	COMPOUND INTEREST	PRESENT VALUE	PRESENT VALUE OF ANNUITY	AMOUNT OF ANNUITY	SINKING FUND
1	1.0200	0.9804	0.9804	1.0000	1.0000
2	1.0404	0.9612	1.9416	2.0200	0.4951
3	1.0612	0.9423	2.8839	3.0604	0.3268
4	1.0824	0.9238	3.8077	4.1216	0.2426
5	1.1041	0.9057	4.7134	5.2040	0.1922
6	1.1262	0.8880	5.6014	6.3081	0.1585
7	1.1487	0.8706	6.4720	7.4343	0.1345
8	1.1717	0.8535	7.3255	8.5829	0.1165
9	1.1951	0.8368	8.1622	9.7546	0.1025
10	1.2190	0.8203	8.9826	10.9497	0.0913
11	1.2434	0.8043	9.7868	12.1687	0.0822
12	1.2682	0.7885	10.5753	13.4120	0.0746
13	1.2936	0.7730	11.3483	14.6803	0.0681
14	1.3195	0.7579	12.1062	15.9739	0.0626
15	1.3459	0.7430	12.8492	17.2934	0.0578
16	1.3728	0.7284	13.5777	18.6392	0.0537
17	1.4002	0.7142	14.2918	20.0120	0.0500
18	1.4282	0.7002	14.9920	21.4122	0.0467
19	1.4568	0.6864	15.6784	22.8405	0.0438
20	1.4859	0.6730	16.3514	24.2973	0.0412
21	1.5157	0.6598	17.0112	25.7832	0.0388
22	1.5460	0.6468	17.6580	27.2989	0.0366
23	1.5769	0.6342	18.2922	28.8449	0.0347
24	1.6084	0.6217	18.9139	30.4218	0.0329
25	1.6406	0.6095	19.5234	32.0302	0.0312
26	1.6734	0.5976	20.1210	33.6708	0.0297
27	1.7069	0.5859	20.7069	35.3442	0.0283
28	1.7410	0.5744	21.2812	37.0511	0.0270
29	1.7758	0.5631	21.8443	38.7921	0.0258
30	1.8114	0.5521	22.3964	40.5679	0.0247
31	1.8476	0.5412	22.9377	42.3793	0.0236
32	1.8845	0.5306	23.4683	44.2269	0.0226
33	1.9222	0.5202	23.9885	46.1114	0.0217
34	1.9607	0.5100	24.4985	48.0336	0.0208
35	1.9999	0.5000	24.9986	49.9943	0.0200
36	2.0399	0.4902	25.4888	51.9942	0.0192
37	2.0807	0.4806	25.9694	54.0340	0.0185
38	2.1223	0.4712	26.4406	56.1147	0.0178
39	2.1647	0.4619	26.9025	58.2370	0.0172
40	2.2080	0.4529	27.3554	60.4017	0.0166
41	2.2522	0.4440	27.7994	62.6098	0.0160
42	2.2972	0.4353	28.2347	64.8620	0.0154
43	2.3432	0.4268	28.6615	67.1592	0.0149
44	2.3900	0.4184	29.0799	69.5024	0.0144
45	2.4378	0.4102	29.4901	71.8924	0.0139
46	2.4866	0.4022	29.8923	74.3302	0.0135
47	2.5363	0.3943	30.2865	76.8168	0.0130
48	2.5871	0.3865	30.6731	79.3532	0.0126
49	2.6388	0.3790	31.0520	81.9402	0.0122
50	2.6916	0.3715	31.4236	84.5790	0.0118

PERIOD	COMPOUND INTEREST	PRESENT VALUE	PRESENT VALUE OF ANNUITY	AMOUNT OF ANNUITY	SINKING FUND
1	1.0250	0.9756	0.9756	1.0000	1.0000
2	1.0506	0.9518	1.9274	2.0250	0.4938
3	1.0769	0.9286	2.8560	3.0756	0.3251
4	1.1038	0.9060	3.7620	4.1525	0.2408
5	1.1314	0.8839	4.6458	5.2563	0.1902
6	1.1597	0.8623	5.5081	6.3877	0.1566
7	1.1887	0.8413	6.3494	7.5474	0.1325
8	1.2184	0.8207	7.1701	8.7361	0.1145
9	1.2489	0.8007	7.9709	9.9545	0.1005
10	1.2801	0.7812	8.7521	11.2034	0.0893
11	1.3121	0.7621	9.5142	12.4835	0.0801
12	1.3449	0.7436	10.2578	13.7955	0.0725
13	1.3785	0.7254	10.9832	15.1404	0.0660
14	1.4130	0.7077	11.6909	16.5189	0.0605
15	1.4483	0.6905	12.3814	17.9319	0.0558
16	1.4845	0.6736	13.0550	19.3802	0.0516
17	1.5216	0.6572	13.7122	20.8647	0.0479
18	1.5597	0.6412	14.3534	22.3863	0.0447
19	1.5986	0.6255	14.9789	23.9460	0.0418
20	1.6386	0.6103	15.5892	25.5446	0.0391
21	1.6796	0.5954	16.1845	27.1832	0.0368
22	1.7216	0.5809	16.7654	28.8628	0.0346
23	1.7646	0.5667	17.3321	30.5844	0.0327
24	1.8087	0.5529	17.8850	32.3490	0.0309
25	1.8539	0.5394	18.4244	34.1577	0.0293
26	1.9003	0.5262	18.9506	36.0117	0.0278
27	1.9478	0.5134	19.4640	37.9120	0.0264
28	1.9965	0.5009	19.9649	39.8598	0.0251
29	2.0464	0.4887	20.4535	41.8563	0.0239
30	2.0976	0.4767	20.9303	43.9027	0.0228
31	2.1500	0.4651	21.3954	46.0002	0.0217
32	2.2038	0.4538	21.8492	48.1502	0.0208
33	2.2588	0.4427	22.2919	50.3540	0.0199
34	2.3153	0.4319	22.7238	52.6128	0.0190
35	2.3732	0.4214	23.1451	54.9282	0.0182
36	2.4325	0.4111	23.5562	57.3014	0.0175
37	2.4933	0.4011	23.9573	59.7339	0.0167
38	2.5557	0.3913	24.3486	62.2272	0.0161
39	2.6196	0.3817	24.7303	64.7829	0.0154
40	2.6851	0.3724	25.1028	67.4025	0.0148
41	2.7522	0.3633	25.4661	70.0875	0.0143
42	2.8210	0.3545	25.8206	72.8397	0.0137
43	2.8915	0.3458	26.1664	75.6607	0.0132
44	2.9638	0.3374	26.5038	78.5522	0.0127
45	3.0379	0.3292	26.8330	81.5160	0.0123
46	3.1138	0.3211	27.1542	84.5539	0.0118
47	3.1917	0.3133	27.4675	87.6678	0.0114
48	3.2715	0.3057	27.7731	90.8595	0.0110
49	3.3533	0.2982	28.0714	94.1310	0.0106
50	3.4371	0.2909	28.3623	97.4842	0.0103

3%

PERIOD	COMPOUND INTEREST	PRESENT VALUE	PRESENT VALUE OF ANNUITY	AMOUNT OF ANNUITY	SINKING FUND
1	1.0300	0.9709	0.9709	1.0000	1.0000
2	1.0609	0.9426	1.9135	2.0300	0.4926
3	1.0927	0.9151	2.8286	3.0909	0.3235
4	1.1255	0.8885	3.7171	4.1836	0.2390
5	1.1593	0.8626	4.5797	5.3091	0.1884
6	1.1941	0.8375	5.4172	6.4684	0.1546
7	1.2299	0.8131	6.2303	7.6625	0.1305
8	1.2668	0.7894	7.0197	8.8923	0.1125
9	1.3048	0.7664	7.7861	10.1591	0.0984
10	1.3439	0.7441	8.5302	11.4639	0.0872
11	1.3842	0.7224	9.2526	12.8078	0.0781
12	1.4258	0.7014	9.9540	14.1920	0.0705
13	1.4685	0.6810	10.6350	15.6178	0.0640
14	1.5126	0.6611	11.2961	17.0863	0.0585
15	1.5580	0.6419	11.9379	18.5989	0.0538
16	1.6047	0.6232	12.5611	20.1569	0.0496
17	1.6528	0.6050	13.1661	21.7616	0.0460
18	1.7024	0.5874	13.7535	23.4144	0.0427
19	1.7535	0.5703	14.3238	25.1169	0.0398
20	1.8061	0.5537	14.8775	26.8704	0.0372
21	1.8603	0.5375	15.4150	28.6765	0.0349
22	1.9161	0.5219	15.9369	30.5368	0.0327
23	1.9736	0.5067	16.4436	32.4529	0.0308
24	2.0328	0.4919	16.9355	34.4265	0.0290
25	2.0938	0.4776	17.4131	36.4593	0.0274
26	2.1566	0.4637	17.8768	38.5530	0.0259
27	2.2213	0.4502	18.3270	40.7096	0.0246
28	2.2879	0.4371	18.7641	42.9309	0.0233
29	2.3566	0.4243	19.1885	45.2188	0.0221
30	2.4273	0.4120	19.6004	47.5754	0.0210
31	2.5001	0.4000	20.0004	50.0027	0.0200
32	2.5751	0.3883	20.3888	52.5027	0.0190
33	2.6523	0.3770	20.7658	55.0778	0.0182
34	2.7319	0.3660	21.1318	57.7302	0.0173
35	2.8139	0.3554	21.4872	60.4621	0.0165
36	2.8983	0.3450	21.8323	63.2759	0.0158
37	2.9852	0.3350	22.1672	66.1742	0.0151
38	3.0748	0.3252	22.4925	69.1594	0.0145
39	3.1670	0.3158	22.8082	72.2342	0.0138
40	3.2620	0.3066	23.1148	75.4012	0.0133
41	3.3599	0.2976	23.4124	78.6633	0.0127
42	3.4607	0.2890	23.7014	82.0232	0.0122
43	3.5645	0.2805	23.9819	85.4839	0.0117
44	3.6715	0.2724	24.2543	89.0484	0.0112
45	3.7816	0.2644	24.5187	92.7198	0.0108
46	3.8950	0.2567	24.7754	96.5014	0.0104
47	4.0119	0.2493	25.0247	100.3965	0.0100
48	4.1323	0.2420	25.2667	104.4084	0.0096
49	4.2562	0.2350	25.5017	108.5406	0.0092
50	4.3839	0.2281	25.7298	112.7968	0.0089

PERIOD	COMPOUND INTEREST	PRESENT VALUE	PRESENT VALUE OF ANNUITY	AMOUNT OF ANNUITY	SINKING FUND
1	1.0350	0.9662	0.9662	1.0000	1.0000
2	1.0712	0.9335	1.8997	2.0350	0.4914
3	1.1087	0.9019	2.8016	3.1062	0.3219
4	1.1475	0.8714	3.6731	4.2149	0.2373
5	1.1877	0.8420	4.5150	5.3625	0.1865
6	1.2293	0.8135	5.3285	6.5501	0.1527
7	1.2723	0.7860	6.1145	7.7794	0.1285
8	1.3168	0.7594	6.8739	9.0517	0.1105
9	1.3629	0.7337	7.6077	10.3685	0.0964
10	1.4106	0.7089	8.3166	11.7314	0.0852
11	1.4600	0.6849	9.0015	13.1420	0.0761
12	1.5111	0.6618	9.6633	14.6019	0.0685
13	1.5640	0.6394	10.3027	16.1130	0.0621
14	1.6187	0.6178	10.9205	17.6770	0.0566
15	1.6753	0.5969	11.5174	19.2957	0.0518
16	1.7340	0.5767	12.0941	20.9710	0.0477
17	1.7947	0.5572	12.6513	22.7050	0.0440
18	1.8575	0.5384	13.1897	24.4997	0.0408
19	1.9225	0.5202	13.7098	26.3571	0.0379
20	1.9898	0.5026	14.2124	28.2796	0.0354
21	2.0594	0.4856	14.6980	30.2694	0.0330
22	2.1315	0.4692	15.1671	32.3288	0.0309
23	2.2061	0.4533	15.6204	34.4604	0.0290
24	2.2833	0.4380	16.0584	36.6665	0.0273
25	2.3632	0.4231	16.4815	38.9498	0.0257
26	2.4460	0.4088	16.8903	41.3130	0.0242
27	2.5316	0.3950	17.2854	43.7590	0.0229
28	2.6202	0.3817	17.6670	46.2905	0.0216
29	2.7119	0.3687	18.0358	48.9107	0.0204
30	2.8068	0.3563	18.3920	51.6226	0.0194
31	2.9050	0.3442	18.7363	54.4294	0.0184
32	3.0067	0.3326	19.0689	57.3344	0.0174
33	3.1119	0.3213	19.3902	60.3411	0.0166
34	3.2209	0.3105	19.7007	63.4530	0.0158
35	3.3336	0.3000	20.0007	66.6739	0.0150
36	3.4503	0.2898	20.2905	70.0075	0.0143
37	3.5710	0.2800	20.5705	73.4577	0.0136
38	3.6960	0.2706	20.8411	77.0287	0.0130
39	3.8254	0.2614	21.1025	80.7247	0.0124
40	3.9593	0.2526	21.3551	84.5501	0.0118
41	4.0978	0.2440	21.5991	88.5093	0.0113
42	4.2413	0.2358	21.8349	92.6072	0.0108
43	4.3897	0.2278	22.0627	96.8484	0.0103
44	4.5433	0.2201	22.2828	101.2381	0.0099
45	4.7023	0.2127	22.4954	105.7814	0.0095
46	4.8669	0.2055	22.7009	110.4838	0.0091
47	5.0373	0.1985	22.8994	115.3507	0.0087
48	5.2136	0.1918	23.0912	120.3880	0.0083
49	5.3961	0.1853	23.2766	125.6015	0.0080
50	5.5849	0.1791	23.4556	130.9976	0.0076

4%

PERIOD	COMPOUND INTEREST	PRESENT VALUE	PRESENT VALUE OF ANNUITY	AMOUNT OF ANNUITY	SINKING FUND
1	1.0400	0.9615	0.9615	1.0000	1.0000
2	1.0816	0.9246	1.8861	2.0400	0.4902
3	1.1249	0.8890	2.7751	3.1216	0.3203
4	1.1699	0.8548	3.6299	4.2465	0.2355
5	1.2167	0.8219	4.4518	5.4163	0.1846
6	1.2653	0.7903	5.2421	6.6330	0.1508
7	1.3159	0.7599	6.0021	7.8983	0.1266
8	1.3686	0.7307	6.7327	9.2142	0.1085
9	1.4233	0.7026	7.4353	10.5828	0.0945
10	1.4802	0.6756	8.1109	12.0061	0.0833
11	1.5395	0.6496	8.7605	13.4863	0.0741
12	1.6010	0.6246	9.3851	15.0258	0.0666
13	1.6651	0.6006	9.9856	16.6268	0.0601
14	1.7317	0.5775	10.5631	18.2919	0.0547
15	1.8009	0.5553	11.1184	20.0236	0.0499
16	1.8730	0.5339	11.6523	21.8245	0.0458
17	1.9479	0.5134	12.1657	23.6975	0.0422
18	2.0258	0.4936	12.6593	25.6454	0.0390
19	2.1068	0.4746	13.1339	27.6712	0.0361
20	2.1911	0.4564	13.5903	29.7781	0.0336
21	2.2788	0.4388	14.0292	31.9692	0.0313
22	2.3699	0.4220	14.4511	34.2479	0.0292
23	2.4647	0.4057	14.8568	36.6179	0.0273
24	2.5633	0.3901	15.2470	39.0826	0.0256
25	2.6658	0.3751	15.6221	41.6459	0.0240
26	2.7725	0.3607	15.9828	44.3117	0.0226
27	2.8834	0.3468	16.3296	47.0842	0.0212
28	2.9987	0.3335	16.6631	49.9675	0.0200
29	3.1187	0.3207	16.9837	52.9662	0.0189
30	3.2434	0.3083	17.2920	56.0849	0.0178
31	3.3731	0.2965	17.5885	59.3283	0.0169
32	3.5081	0.2851	17.8735	62.7014	0.0159
33	3.6484	0.2741	18.1476	66.2095	0.0151
34	3.7943	0.2636	18.4112	69.8578	0.0143
35	3.9461	0.2534	18.6646	73.6521	0.0136
36	4.1039	0.2437	18.9083	77.5982	0.0129
37	4.2681	0.2343	19.1426	81.7022	0.0122
38	4.4388	0.2253	19.3679	85.9702	0.0116
39	4.6164	0.2166	19.5845	90.4091	0.0111
40	4.8010	0.2083	19.7928	95.0254	0.0105
41	4.9931	0.2003	19.9930	99.8264	0.0100
42	5.1928	0.1926	20.1856	104.8195	0.0095
43	5.4005	0.1852	20.3708	110.0122	0.0091
44	5.6165	0.1780	20.5488	115.4127	0.0087
45	5.8412	0.1712	20.7200	121.0292	0.0083
46	6.0748	0.1646	20.8847	126.8704	0.0079
47	6.3178	0.1583	21.0429	132.9452	0.0075
48	6.5705	0.1522	21.1951	139.2630	0.0072
49	6.8333	0.1463	21.3415	145.8335	0.0069
50	7.1067	0.1407	21.4822	152.6669	0.0066

PERIOD	COMPOUND INTEREST	PRESENT VALUE	PRESENT VALUE OF ANNUITY	AMOUNT OF ANNUITY	SINKING FUND
1	1.0450	0.9569	0.9569	1.0000	1.0000
2	1.0920	0.9157	1.8727	2.0450	0.4890
3	1.1412	0.8763	2.7490	3.1370	0.3188
4	1.1925	0.8386	3.5875	4.2782	0.2337
5	1.2462	0.8025	4.3900	5.4707	0.1828
6	1.3023	0.7679	5.1579	6.7169	0.1489
7	1.3609	0.7348	5.8927	8.0191	0.1247
8	1.4221	0.7032	6.5959	9.3800	0.1066
9	1.4861	0.6729	7.2688	10.8021	0.0926
10	1.5530	0.6439	7.9127	12.2882	0.0814
11	1.6229	0.6162	8.5289	13.8412	0.0722
12	1.6959	0.5897	9.1186	15.4640	0.0647
13	1.7722	0.5643	9.6828	17.1599	0.0583
14	1.8519	0.5400	10.2228	18.9321	0.0528
15	1.9353	0.5167	10.7395	20.7840	0.0481
16	2.0224	0.4945	11.2340	22.7193	0.0440
17	2.1134	0.4732	11.7072	24.7417	0.0404
18	2.2085	0.4528	12.1600	26.8551	0.0372
19	2.3079	0.4333	12.5933	29.0635	0.0344
20	2.4117	0.4146	13.0079	31.3714	0.0319
21	2.5202	0.3968	13.4047	33.7831	0.0296
22	2.6337	0.3797	13.7844	36.3033	0.0275
23	2.7522	0.3634	14.1478	38.9370	0.0257
24	2.8760	0.3477	14.4955	41.6892	0.0240
25	3.0054	0.3327	14.8282	44.5652	0.0224
26	3.1407	0.3184	15.1466	47.5706	0.0210
27	3.2820	0.3047	15.4513	50.7113	0.0197
28	3.4297	0.2916	15.7429	53.9933	0.0185
29	3.5840	0.2790	16.0219	57.4230	0.0174
30	3.7453	0.2670	16.2889	61.0070	0.0164
31	3.9139	0.2555	16.5444	64.7523	0.0154
32	4.0900	0.2445	16.7889	68.6662	0.0146
33	4.2740	0.2340	17.0229	72.7562	0.0137
34	4.4664	0.2239	17.2468	77.0302	0.0130
35	4.6673	0.2143	17.4610	81.4965	0.0123
36	4.8774	0.2050	17.6660	86.1639	0.0116
37	5.0969	0.1962	17.8622	91.0412	0.0110
38	5.3262	0.1878	18.0500	96.1381	0.0104
39	5.5659	0.1797	18.2297	101.4643	0.0099
40	5.8164	0.1719	18.4016	107.0302	0.0093
41	6.0781	0.1645	18.5661	112.8466	0.0089
42	6.3516	0.1574	18.7235	118.9247	0.0084
43	6.6374	0.1507	18.8742	125.2763	0.0080
44	6.9361	0.1442	19.0184	131.9137	0.0076
45	7.2482	0.1380	19.1563	138.8498	0.0072
46	7.5744	0.1320	19.2884	146.0980	0.0068
47	7.9153	0.1263	19.4147	153.6724	0.0065
48	8.2714	0.1209	19.5356	161.5877	0.0062
49	8.6437	0.1157	19.6513	169.8592	0.0059
50	9.0326	0.1107	19.7620	178.5028	0.0056

5%

PERIOD	COMPOUND INTEREST	PRESENT VALUE	PRESENT VALUE OF ANNUITY	AMOUNT OF ANNUITY	SINKING FUND
1	1.0500	0.9524	0.9524	1.0000	1.0000
2	1.1025	0.9070	1.8594	2.0500	0.4878
3	1.1576	0.8638	2.7232	3.1525	0.3172
4	1.2155	0.8227	3.5459	4.3101	0.2320
5	1.2763	0.7835	4.3295	5.5256	0.1810
6	1.3401	0.7462	5.0757	6.8019	0.1470
7	1.4071	0.7107	5.7864	8.1420	0.1228
8	1.4775	0.6768	6.4632	9.5491	0.1047
9	1.5513	0.6446	7.1078	11.0265	0.0907
10	1.6289	0.6139	7.7217	12.5779	0.0795
11	1.7103	0.5847	8.3064	14.2068	0.0704
12	1.7959	0.5568	8.8632	15.9171	0.0628
13	1.8856	0.5303	9.3936	17.7129	0.0565
14	1.9799	0.5051	9.8986	19.5986	0.0510
15	2.0789	0.4810	10.3796	21.5785	0.0463
16	2.1829	0.4581	10.8378	23.6574	0.0423
17	2.2920	0.4363	11.2741	25.8403	0.0387
18	2.4066	0.4155	11.6896	28.1323	0.0355
19	2.5270	0.3957	12.0853	30.5389	0.0327
20	2.6533	0.3769	12.4622	33.0659	0.0302
21	2.7860	0.3589	12.8211	35.7192	0.0280
22	2.9253	0.3418	13.1630	38.5051	0.0260
23	3.0715	0.3256	13.4886	41.4304	0.0241
24	3.2251	0.3101	13.7986	44.5019	0.0225
25	3.3864	0.2953	14.0939	47.7270	0.0210
26	3.5557	0.2812	14.3752	51.1133	0.0196
27	3.7335	0.2678	14.6430	54.6690	0.0183
28	3.9201	0.2551	14.8981	58.4024	0.0171
29	4.1161	0.2429	15.1411	62.3225	0.0160
30	4.3219	0.2314	15.3724	66.4386	0.0151
31	4.5380	0.2204	15.5928	70.7606	0.0141
32	4.7649	0.2099	15.8027	75.2986	0.0133
33	5.0032	0.1999	16.0025	80.0635	0.0125
34	5.2533	0.1904	16.1929	85.0667	0.0118
35	5.5160	0.1813	16.3742	90.3200	0.0111
36	5.7918	0.1727	16.5468	95.8360	0.0104
37	6.0814	0.1644	16.7113	101.6278	0.0098
38	6.3855	0.1566	16.8679	107.7092	0.0093
39	6.7047	0.1491	17.0170	114.0946	0.0088
40	7.0400	0.1420	17.1591	120.7993	0.0083
41	7.3920	0.1353	17.2944	127.8393	0.0078
42	7.7616	0.1288	17.4232	135.2312	0.0074
43	8.1496	0.1227	17.5459	142.9928	0.0070
44	8.5571	0.1169	17.6628	151.1424	0.0066
45	8.9850	0.1113	17.7741	159.6995	0.0063
46	9.4342	0.1060	17.8801	168.6845	0.0059
47	9.9059	0.1009	17.9810	178.1187	0.0056
48	10.4012	0.0961	18.0772	188.0246	0.0053
49	10.9213	0.0916	18.1687	198.4258	0.0050
50	11.4674	0.0872	18.2559	209.3470	0.0048

PERIOD	COMPOUND INTEREST	PRESENT VALUE	PRESENT VALUE OF ANNUITY	AMOUNT OF ANNUITY	SINKING FUND
1	1.0550	0.9479	0.9479	1.0000	1.0000
2	1.1130	0.8985	1.8463	2.0550	0.4866
3	1.1742	0.8516	2.6979	3.1680	0.3157
4	1.2388	0.8072	3.5051	4.3423	0.2303
5	1.3070	0.7651	4.2703	5.5811	0.1792
6	1.3788	0.7252	4.9955	6.8880	0.1452
7	1.4547	0.6874	5.6830	8.2669	0.1210
8	1.5347	0.6516	6.3346	9.7216	0.1029
9	1.6191	0.6176	6.9522	11.2562	0.0888
10	1.7081	0.5854	7.5376	12.8753	0.0777
11	1.8021	0.5549	8.0925	14.5835	0.0686
12	1.9012	0.5260	8.6185	16.3856	0.0610
13	2.0058	0.4986	9.1171	18.2868	0.0547
14	2.1161	0.4726	9.5896	20.2925	0.0493
15	2.2325	0.4479	10.0376	22.4086	0.0446
16	2.3553	0.4246	10.4622	24.6411	0.0406
17	2.4848	0.4024	10.8646	26.9963	0.0370
18	2.6215	0.3815	11.2461	29.4811	0.0339
19	2.7656	0.3616	11.6076	32.1026	0.0312
20	2.9178	0.3427	11.9504	34.8682	0.0287
21	3.0782	0.3249	12.2752	37.7860	0.0265
22	3.2475	0.3079	12.5832	40.8642	0.0245
23	3.4261	0.2919	12.8750	44.1117	0.0227
24	3.6146	0.2767	13.1517	47.5379	0.0210
25	3.8134	0.2622	13.4139	51.1524	0.0195
26	4.0231	0.2486	13.6625	54.9658	0.0182
27	4.2444	0.2356	13.8981	58.9889	0.0170
28	4.4778	0.2233	14.1214	63.2333	0.0158
29	4.7241	0.2117	14.3331	67.7112	0.0148
30	4.9839	0.2006	14.5337	72.4353	0.0138
31	5.2581	0.1902	14.7239	77.4192	0.0129
32	5.5472	0.1803	14.9042	82.6772	0.0121
33	5.8523	0.1709	15.0751	88.2245	0.0113
34	6.1742	0.1620	15.2370	94.0768	0.0106
35	6.5138	0.1535	15.3905	100.2510	0.0100
36	6.8721	0.1455	15.5361	106.7648	0.0094
37	7.2500	0.1379	15.6740	113.6369	0.0088
38	7.6488	0.1307	15.8047	120.8869	0.0083
39	8.0695	0.1239	15.9287	128.5357	0.0078
40	8.5133	0.1175	16.0461	136.6051	0.0073
41	8.9815	0.1113	16.1575	145.1184	0.0069
42	9.4755	0.1055	16.2630	154.0999	0.0065
43	9.9966	0.1000	16.3630	163.5753	0.0061
44	10.5465	0.0948	16.4578	173.5720	0.0058
45	11.1265	0.0899	16.5477	184.1184	0.0054
46	11.7385	0.0852	16.6329	195.2449	0.0051
47	12.3841	0.0807	16.7137	206.9834	0.0048
48	13.0652	0.0765	16.7902	219.3674	0.0046
49	13.7838	0.0725	16.8627	232.4326	0.0043
50	14.5419	0.0688	16.9315	246.2164	0.0041

6%

PERIOD	COMPOUND INTEREST	PRESENT VALUE	PRESENT VALUE OF ANNUITY	AMOUNT OF ANNUITY	SINKING FUND
1	1.0600	0.9434	0.9434	1.0000	1.0000
2	1.1236	0.8900	1.8334	2.0600	0.4854
3	1.1910	0.8396	2.6730	3.1836	0.3141
4	1.2625	0.7921	3.4651	4.3746	0.2286
5	1.3382	0.7473	4.2124	5.6371	0.1774
6	1.4185	0.7050	4.9173	6.9753	0.1434
7	1.5036	0.6651	5.5824	8.3938	0.1191
8	1.5938	0.6274	6.2098	9.8975	0.1010
9	1.6895	0.5919	6.8017	11.4913	0.0870
10	1.7908	0.5584	7.3601	13.1808	0.0759
11	1.8983	0.5268	7.8869	14.9716	0.0668
12	2.0122	0.4970	8.3838	16.8699	0.0593
13	2.1329	0.4688	8.8527	18.8821	0.0530
14	2.2609	0.4423	9.2950	21.0150	0.0476
15	2.3966	0.4173	9.7122	23.2759	0.0430
16	2.5404	0.3936	10.1059	25.6725	0.0390
17	2.6928	0.3714	10.4773	28.2128	0.0354
18	2.8543	0.3503	10.8276	30.9056	0.0324
19	3.0256	0.3305	11.1581	33.7599	0.0296
20	3.2071	0.3118	11.4699	36.7855	0.0272
21	3.3996	0.2942	11.7641	39.9927	0.0250
22	3.6035	0.2775	12.0416	43.3922	0.0230
23	3.8197	0.2618	12.3034	46.9958	0.0213
24	4.0489	0.2470	12.5504	50.8155	0.0197
25	4.2919	0.2330	12.7834	54.8644	0.0182
26	4.5494	0.2198	13.0032	59.1563	0.0169
27	4.8223	0.2074	13.2105	63.7057	0.0157
28	5.1117	0.1956	13.4062	68.5280	0.0146
29	5.4184	0.1846	13.5907	73.6397	0.0136
30	5.7435	0.1741	13.7648	79.0580	0.0126
31	6.0881	0.1643	13.9291	84.8015	0.0118
32	6.4534	0.1550	14.0840	90.8896	0.0110
33	6.8406	0.1462	14.2302	97.3430	0.0103
34	7.2510	0.1379	14.3681	104.1836	0.0096
35	7.6861	0.1301	14.4982	111.4346	0.0090
36	8.1472	0.1227	14.6210	119.1206	0.0084
37	8.6361	0.1158	14.7368	127.2679	0.0079
38	9.1542	0.1092	14.8460	135.9039	0.0074
39	9.7035	0.1031	14.9491	145.0581	0.0069
40	10.2857	0.0972	15.0463	154.7616	0.0065
41	10.9028	0.0917	15.1380	165.0473	0.0061
42	11.5570	0.0865	15.2245	175.9501	0.0057
43	12.2504	0.0816	15.3062	187.5071	0.0053
44	12.9855	0.0770	15.3832	199.7575	0.0050
45	13.7646	0.0727	15.4558	212.7430	0.0047
46	14.5905	0.0685	15.5244	226.5076	0.0044
47	15.4659	0.0647	15.5890	241.0980	0.0041
48	16.3938	0.0610	15.6500	256.5639	0.0039
49	17.3775	0.0575	15.7076	272.9577	0.0037
50	18.4201	0.0543	15.7619	290.3351	0.0034

PERIOD	COMPOUND INTEREST	PRESENT VALUE	PRESENT VALUE OF ANNUITY	AMOUNT OF ANNUITY	SINKING FUND
1	1.0650	0.9390	0.9390	1.0000	1.0000
2	1.1342	0.8817	1.8206	2.0650	0.4843
3	1.2079	0.8278	2.6485	3.1992	0.3126
4	1.2865	0.7773	3.4258	4.4072	0.2269
5	1.3701	0.7299	4.1557	5.6936	0.1756
6	1.4591	0.6853	4.8410	7.0637	0.1416
7	1.5540	0.6435	5.4845	8.5229	0.1173
8	1.6550	0.6042	6.0887	10.0768	0.0992
9	1.7626	0.5674	6.6561	11.7318	0.0852
10	1.8771	0.5327	7.1888	13.4944	0.0741
11	1.9992	0.5002	7.6890	15.3715	0.0651
12	2.1291	0.4697	8.1587	17.3707	0.0576
13	2.2675	0.4410	8.5997	19.4998	0.0513
14	2.4149	0.4141	9.0138	21.7673	0.0459
15	2.5718	0.3888	9.4027	24.1821	0.0414
16	2.7390	0.3651	9.7678	26.7540	0.0374
17	2.9170	0.3428	10.1106	29.4930	0.0339
18	3.1067	0.3219	10.4325	32.4100	0.0309
19	3.3086	0.3022	10.7347	35.5167	0.0282
20	3.5236	0.2838	11.0185	38.8253	0.0258
21	3.7527	0.2665	11.2850	42.3489	0.0236
22	3.9966	0.2502	11.5352	46.1016	0.0217
23	4.2564	0.2349	11.7701	50.0982	0.0200
24	4.5330	0.2206	11.9907	54.3546	0.0184
25	4.8277	0.2071	12.1979	58.8876	0.0170
26	5.1415	0.1945	12.3924	63.7153	0.0157
27	5.4757	0.1826	12.5750	68.8568	0.0145
28	5.8316	0.1715	12.7465	74.3325	0.0135
29	6.2107	0.1610	12.9075	80.1641	0.0125
30	6.6144	0.1512	13.0587	86.3747	0.0116
31	7.0443	0.1420	13.2006	92.9891	0.0108
32	7.5022	0.1333	13.3339	100.0334	0.0100
33	7.9898	0.1252	13.4591	107.5355	0.0093
34	8.5091	0.1175	13.5766	115.5254	0.0087
35	9.0622	0.1103	13.6870	124.0345	0.0081
36	9.6513	0.1036	13.7906	133.0967	0.0075
37	10.2786	0.0973	13.8879	142.7480	0.0070
38	10.9467	0.0914	13.9792	153.0266	0.0065
39	11.6583	0.0858	14.0650	163.9733	0.0061
40	12.4161	0.0805	14.1455	175.6316	0.0057
41	13.2231	0.0756	14.2212	188.0476	0.0053
42	14.0826	0.0710	14.2922	201.2707	0.0050
43	14.9980	0.0667	14.3588	215.3533	0.0046
44	15.9728	0.0626	14.4214	230.3513	0.0043
45	17.0111	0.0588	14.4802	246.3241	0.0041
46	18.1168	0.0552	14.5354	263.3352	0.0038
47	19.2944	0.0518	14.5873	281.4519	0.0036
48	20.5485	0.0487	14.6359	300.7463	0.0033
49	21.8842	0.0457	14.6816	321.2948	0.0031
50	23.3066	0.0429	14.7245	343.1789	0.0029

7%

PERIOD	COMPOUND INTEREST	PRESENT VALUE	PRESENT VALUE OF ANNUITY	AMOUNT OF ANNUITY	SINKING FUND
1	1.0700	0.9346	0.9346	1.0000	1.0000
2	1.1449	0.8734	1.8080	2.0700	0.4831
3	1.2250	0.8163	2.6243	3.2149	0.3111
4	1.3108	0.7629	3.3872	4.4399	0.2252
5	1.4026	0.7130	4.1002	5.7507	0.1739
6	1.5007	0.6663	4.7665	7.1533	0.1398
7	1.6058	0.6227	5.3893	8.6540	0.1156
8	1.7182	0.5820	5.9713	10.2598	0.0975
9	1.8385	0.5439	6.5152	11.9780	0.0835
10	1.9672	0.5083	7.0236	13.8164	0.0724
11	2.1049	0.4751	7.4987	15.7836	0.0634
12	2.2522	0.4440	7.9427	17.8884	0.0559
13	2.4098	0.4150	8.3576	20.1406	0.0497
14	2.5785	0.3878	8.7455	22.5505	0.0443
15	2.7590	0.3624	9.1079	25.1290	0.0398
16	2.9522	0.3387	9.4466	27.8880	0.0359
17	3.1588	0.3166	9.7632	30.8402	0.0324
18	3.3799	0.2959	10.0591	33.9990	0.0294
19	3.6165	0.2765	10.3356	37.3789	0.0268
20	3.8697	0.2584	10.5940	40.9954	0.0244
21	4.1406	0.2415	10.8355	44.8651	0.0223
22	4.4304	0.2257	11.0612	49.0057	0.0204
23	4.7405	0.2109	11.2722	53.4360	0.0187
24	5.0724	0.1971	11.4693	58.1766	0.0172
25	5.4274	0.1842	11.6536	63.2489	0.0158
26	5.8074	0.1722	11.8258	68.6763	0.0146
27	6.2139	0.1609	11.9867	74.4837	0.0134
28	6.6488	0.1504	12.1371	80.6975	0.0124
29	7.1143	0.1406	12.2777	87.3464	0.0114
30	7.6123	0.1314	12.4090	94.4606	0.0106
31	8.1451	0.1228	12.5318	102.0728	0.0098
32	8.7153	0.1147	12.6466	110.2179	0.0091
33	9.3253	0.1072	12.7538	118.9332	0.0084
34	9.9781	0.1002	12.8540	128.2585	0.0078
35	10.6766	0.0937	12.9477	138.2366	0.0072
36	11.4239	0.0875	13.0352	148.9131	0.0067
37	12.2236	0.0818	13.1170	160.3370	0.0062
38	13.0792	0.0765	13.1935	172.5606	0.0058
39	13.9948	0.0715	13.2649	185.6398	0.0054
40	14.9744	0.0668	13.3317	199.6346	0.0050
41	16.0226	0.0624	13.3941	214.6090	0.0047
42	17.1442	0.0583	13.4524	230.6317	0.0043
43	18.3443	0.0545	13.5070	247.7758	0.0040
44	19.6284	0.0509	13.5579	266.1201	0.0038
45	21.0024	0.0476	13.6055	285.7485	0.0035
46	22.4726	0.0445	13.6500	306.7509	0.0033
47	24.0456	0.0416	13.6916	329.2234	0.0030
48	25.7288	0.0389	13.7305	353.2691	0.0028
49	27.5298	0.0363	13.7668	378.9978	0.0026
50	29.4569	0.0339	13.8007	406.5277	0.0025

PERIOD	COMPOUND INTEREST	PRESENT VALUE	PRESENT VALUE OF ANNUITY	AMOUNT OF ANNUITY	SINKING FUND
1	1.0750	0.9302	0.9302	1.0000	1.0000
2	1.1556	0.8653	1.7956	2.0750	0.4819
3	1.2423	0.8050	2.6005	3.2306	0.3095
4	1.3355	0.7488	3.3493	4.4729	0.2236
5	1.4356	0.6966	4.0459	5.8084	0.1722
6	1.5433	0.6480	4.6938	7.2440	0.1380
7	1.6590	0.6028	5.2966	8.7873	0.1138
8	1.7835	0.5607	5.8573	10.4464	0.0957
9	1.9172	0.5216	6.3789	12.2299	0.0818
10	2.0610	0.4852	6.8641	14.1471	0.0707
11	2.2156	0.4513	7.3154	16.2081	0.0617
12	2.3818	0.4199	7.7353	18.4237	0.0543
13	2.5604	0.3906	8.1258	20.8055	0.0481
14	2.7524	0.3633	8.4892	23.3659	0.0428
15	2.9589	0.3380	8.8271	26.1184	0.0383
16	3.1808	0.3144	9.1415	29.0773	0.0344
17	3.4194	0.2925	9.4340	32.2581	0.0310
18	3.6758	0.2720	9.7060	35.6774	0.0280
19	3.9515	0.2531	9.9591	39.3532	0.0254
20	4.2479	0.2354	10.1945	43.3047	0.0231
21	4.5664	0.2190	10.4135	47.5526	0.0210
22	4.9089	0.2037	10.6172	52.1190	0.0192
23	5.2771	0.1895	10.8067	57.0280	0.0175
24	5.6729	0.1763	10.9830	62.3051	0.0161
25	6.0983	0.1640	11.1469	67.9780	0.0147
26	6.5557	0.1525	11.2995	74.0763	0.0135
27	7.0474	0.1419	11.4414	80.6320	0.0124
28	7.5760	0.1320	11.5734	87.6794	0.0114
29	8.1442	0.1228	11.6962	95.2554	0.0105
30	8.7550	0.1142	11.8104	103.3996	0.0097
31	9.4116	0.1063	11.9166	112.1545	0.0089
32	10.1175	0.0988	12.0155	121.5661	0.0082
33	10.8763	0.0919	12.1074	131.6836	0.0076
34	11.6920	0.0855	12.1930	142.5599	0.0070
35.	12.5689	0.0796	12.2725	154.2519	0.0065
36	13.5116	0.0740	12.3465	166.8208	0.0060
37	14.5249	0.0688	12.4154	180.3323	0.0055
38	15.6143	0.0640	12.4794	194.8573	0.0051
39	16.7854	0.0596	12.5390	210.4716	0.0048
40	18.0443	0.0554	12.5944	227.2569	0.0044
41	19.3976	0.0516	12.6460	245.3012	0.0041
42	20.8524	0.0480	12.6939	264.6988	0.0038
43	22.4163	0.0446	12.7385	285.5513	0.0035
44	24.0976	0.0415	12.7800	307.9676	0.0032
45	25.9049	0.0386	12.8186	332.0652	0.0030
46	27.8478	0.0359	12.8545	357.9701	0.0028
47	29.9363	0.0334	12.8879	385.8179	0.0026
48	32.1816	0.0311	12.9190	415.7542	0.0024
49	34.5952	0.0289	12.9479	447.9358	0.0022
50	37.1898	0.0269	12.9748	482.5310	0.0021

8%

PERIOD	COMPOUND INTEREST	PRESENT VALUE	PRESENT VALUE OF ANNUITY	AMOUNT OF ANNUITY	SINKING FUND
1	1.0800	0.9259	0.9259	1.0000	1.0000
2	1.1664	0.8573	1.7833	2.0800	0.4808
3	1.2597	0.7938	2.5771	3.2464	0.3080
4	1.3605	0.7350	3.3121	4.5061	0.2219
5	1.4693	0.6806	3.9927	5.8666	0.1705
6	1.5869	0.6302	4.6229	7.3359	0.1363
7	1.7138	0.5835	5.2064	8.9228	0.1121
8	1.8509	0.5403	5.7466	10.6366	0.0940
9	1.9990	0.5002	6.2469	12.4876	0.0801
10	2.1589	0.4632	6.7101	14.4866	0.0690
11	2.3316	0.4289	7.1390	16.6455	0.0601
12	2.5182	0.3971	7.5361	18.9771	0.0527
13	2.7196	0.3677	7.9038	21.4953	0.0465
14	2.9372	0.3405	8.2442	24.2149	0.0413
15	3.1722	0.3152	8.5595	27.1521	0.0368
16	3.4259	0.2919	8.8514	30.3243	0.0330
17	3.7000	0.2703	9.1216	33.7503	0.0296
18	3.9960	0.2502	9.3719	37.4503	0.0267
19	4.3157	0.2317	9.6036	41.4463	0.0241
20	4.6610	0.2145	9.8181	45.7620	0.0219
21	5.0338	0.1987	10.0168	50.4230	0.0198
22	5.4365	0.1839	10.2007	55.4568	0.0180
23	5.8715	0.1703	10.3711	60.8933	0.0164
24	6.3412	0.1577	10.5288	66.7648	0.0150
25	6.8485	0.1460	10.6748	73.1060	0.0137
26	7.3964	0.1352	10.8100	79.9545	0.0125
27	7.9881	0.1252	10.9352	87.3509	0.0114
28	8.6271	0.1159	11.0511	95.3389	0.0105
29	9.3173	0.1073	11.1584	103.9660	0.0096
30	10.0627	0.0994	11.2578	113.2833	0.0088
31	10.8677	0.0920	11.3498	123.3460	0.0081
32	11.7371	0.0852	11.4350	134.2137	0.0075
33	12.6761	0.0789	11.5139	145.9508	0.0069
34	13.6901	0.0730	11.5869	158.6269	0.0063
35	14.7854	0.0676	11.6546	172.3170	0.0058
36	15.9682	0.0626	11.7172	187.1024	0.0053
37	17.2456	0.0580	11.7752	203.0706	0.0049
38	18.6253	0.0537	11.8289	220.3162	0.0045
39	20.1153	0.0497	11.8786	238.9415	0.0042
40	21.7245	0.0460	11.9246	259.0569	0.0039
41	23.4625	0.0426	11.9672	280.7814	0.0036
42	25.3395	0.0395	12.0067	304.2440	0.0033
43	27.3667	0.0365	12.0432	329.5835	0.0030
44	29.5560	0.0338	12.0771	356.9502	0.0028
45	31.9205	0.0313	12.1084	386.5062	0.0026
46	34.4741	0.0290	12.1374	418.4267	0.0024
47	37.2321	0.0269	12.1643	452.9009	0.0022
48	40.2106	0.0249	12.1891	490.1329	0.0020
49	43.4275	0.0230	12.2122	530.3436	0.0019
50	46.9017	0.0213	12.2335	573.7711	0.0017

PERIOD	COMPOUND INTEREST	PRESENT VALUE	PRESENT VALUE OF ANNUITY	AMOUNT OF ANNUITY	SINKING FUND
1	1.0850	0.9217	0.9217	1.0000	1.0000
2	1.1772	0.8495	1.7711	2.0850	0.4796
3	1.2773	0.7829	2.5540	3.2622	0.3065
4	1.3859	0.7216	3.2756	4.5395	0.2203
5	1.5037	0.6650	3.9406	5.9254	0.1688
6	1.6315	0.6129	4.5536	7.4290	0.1346
7	1.7701	0.5649	5.1185	9.0605	0.1104
8	1.9206	0.5207	5.6392	10.8307	0.0923
9	2.0839	0.4799	6.1191	12.7513	0.0784
10	2.2610	0.4423	6.5614	14.8351	0.0674
11	2.4532	0.4076	6.9690	17.0961	0.0585
12	2.6617	0.3757	7.3447	19.5493	0.0512
13	2.8879	0.3463	7.6910	22.2110	0.0450
14	3.1334	0.3191	8.0101	25.0989	0.0398
15	3.3997	0.2941	8.3042	28.2323	0.0354
16	3.6887	0.2711	8.5753	31.6321	0.0316
17	4.0023	0.2499	8.8252	35.3208	0.0283
18	4.3425	0.2303	9.0555	39.3230	0.0254
19	4.7116	0.2122	9.2677	43.6655	0.0229
20	5.1121	0.1956	9.4633	48.3771	0.0207
21	5.5466	0.1803	9.6436	53.4891	0.0187
22	6.0180	0.1662	9.8098	59.0357	0.0169
23	6.5296	0.1531	9.9629	65.0538	0.0154
24	7.0846	0.1412	10.1041	71.5833	0.0140
25	7.6868	0.1301	10.2342	78.6679	0.0127
26	8.3401	0.1199	10.3541	86.3547	0.0116
27	9.0491	0.1105	10.4646	94.6949	0.0106
28	9.8182	0.1019	10.5665	103.7439	0.0096
29	10.6528	0.0939	10.6603	113.5622	0.0088
30	11.5583	0.0865	10.7468	124.2149	0.0081
31	12.5407	0.0797	10.8266	135.7732	0.0074
32	13.6067	0.0735	10.9001	148.3140	0.0067
33	14.7633	0.0677	10.9678	161.9207	0.0062
34	16.0181	0.0624	11.0302	176.6839	0.0057
35	17.3797	0.0575	11.0878	192.7021	0.0052
36	18.8569	0.0530	11.1408	210.0818	0.0048
37	20.4598	0.0489	11.1897	228.9387	0.0044
38	22.1989	0.0450	11.2347	249.3985	0.0040
39	24.0858	0.0415	11.2763	271.5974	0.0037
40	26.1331	0.0383	11.3145	295.6832	0.0034
41	28.3544	0.0353	11.3498	321.8163	0.0031
42	30.7645	0.0325	11.3823	350.1707	0.0029
43	33.3795	0.0300	11.4123	380.9352	0.0026
44	36.2168	0.0276	11.4399	414.3148	0.0024
45	39.2952	0.0254	11.4653	450.5315	0.0022
46	42.6353	0.0235	11.4888	489.8267	0.0020
47	46.2593	0.0216	11.5104	532.4620	0.0019
48	50.1913	0.0199	11.5303	578.7213	0.0017
49	54.4576	0.0184	11.5487	628.9127	0.0016
50	59.0865	0.0169	11.5656	683.3703	0.0015

9%

PERIOD	COMPOUND INTEREST	PRESENT VALUE	PRESENT VALUE OF ANNUITY	AMOUNT OF ANNUITY	SINKING FUND
1	1.0900	0.9174	0.9174	1.0000	1.0000
2	1.1881	0.8417	1.7591	2.0900	0.4785
3	1.2950	0.7722	2.5313	3.2781	0.3051
4	1.4116	0.7084	3.2397	4.5731	0.2187
5	1.5386	0.6499	3.8897	5.9847	0.1671
6	1.6771	0.5963	4.4859	7.5233	0.1329
7	1.8280	0.5470	5.0330	9.2004	0.1087
8	1.9926	0.5019	5.5348	11.0285	0.0907
9	2.1719	0.4604	5.9952	13.0210	0.0768
10	2.3674	0.4224	6.4177	15.1929	0.0658
11	2.5804	0.3875	6.8052	17.5603	0.0569
12	2.8127	0.3555	7.1607	20.1407	0.0497
13	3.0658	0.3262	7.4869	22.9534	0.0436
14	3.3417	0.2992	7.7862	26.0192	0.0384
15	3.6425	0.2745	8.0607	29.3609	0.0341
16	3.9703	0.2519	8.3126	33.0034	0.0303
17	4.3276	0.2311	8.5436	36.9737	0.0270
18	4.7171	0.2120	8.7556	41.3014	0.0242
19	5.1417	0.1945	8.9501	46.0185	0.0217
20	5.6044	0.1784	9.1285	51.1602	0.0195
21	6.1088	0.1637	9.2922	56.7646	0.0176
22	6.6586	0.1502	9.4424	62.8734	0.0159
23	7.2579	0.1378	9.5802	69.5320	0.0144
24	7.9111	0.1264	9.7066	76.7899	0.0130
25	8.6231	0.1160	9.8226	84.7010	0.0118
26	9.3992	0.1064	9.9290	93.3241	0.0107
27	10.2451	0.0976	10.0266	102.7233	0.0097
28	11.1672	0.0895	10.1161	112.9684	0.0089
29	12.1722	0.0822	10.1983	124.1355	0.0081
30	13.2677	0.0754	10.2737	136.3077	0.0073
31	14.4618	0.0691	10.3428	149.5754	0.0067
32	15.7634	0.0634	10.4062	164.0372	0.0061
33	17.1821	0.0582	10.4644	179.8006	0.0056
34	18.7284	0.0534	10.5178	196.9827	0.0051
35	20.4140	0.0490	10.5668	215.7111	0.0046
36	22.2513	0.0449	10.6118	236.1251	0.0042
37	24.2539	0.0412	10.6530	258.3764	0.0039
38	26.4367	0.0378	10.6908	282.6303	0.0035
39	28.8160	0.0347	10.7255	309.0670	0.0032
40	31.4095	0.0318	10.7574	337.8831	0.0030
41	34.2363	0.0292	10.7866	369.2925	0.0027
42	37.3176	0.0268	10.8134	403.5289	0.0025
43	40.6762	0.0246	10.8380	440.8465	0.0023
44	44.3371	0.0226	10.8605	481.5228	0.0021
45	48.3274	0.0207	10.8812	525.8598	0.0019
46	52.6769	0.0190	10.9002	574.1872	0.0017
47	57.4178	0.0174	10.9176	626.8641	0.0016
48	62.5854	0.0160	10.9336	684.2819	0.0015
49	68.2181	0.0147	10.9482	746.8673	0.0013
50	74.3577	0.0134	10.9617	815.0853	0.0012

PERIOD	COMPOUND INTEREST	PRESENT VALUE	PRESENT VALUE OF ANNUITY	AMOUNT OF ANNUITY	SINKING FUND
1	1.0950	0.9132	0.9132	1.0000	1.0000
2	1.1990	0.8340	1.7473	2.0950	0.4773
3	1.3129	0.7617	2.5089	3.2940	0.3036
4	1.4377	0.6956	3.2045	4.6070	0.2171
5	1.5742	0.6352	3.8397	6.0446	0.1654
6	1.7238	0.5801	4.4198	7.6189	0.1313
7	1.8876	0.5298	4.9496	9.3427	0.1070
8	2.0669	0.4838	5.4334	11.2302	0.0890
9	2.2632	0.4418	5.8753	13.2971	0.0752
10	2.4782	0.4035	6.2788	15.5603	0.0643
11	2.7137	0.3685	6.6473	18.0385	0.0554
12	2.9715	0.3365	6.9838	20.7522	0.0482
13	3.2537	0.3073	7.2912	23.7236	0.0422
14	3.5629	0.2807	7.5719	26.9774	0.0371
15	3.9013	0.2563	7.8282	30.5402	0.0327
16	4.2719	0.2341	8.0623	34.4416	0.0290
17	4.6778	0.2138	8.2760	38.7135	0.0258
18	5.1222	0.1952	8.4713	43.3913	0.0230
19	5.6088	0.1783	8.6496	48.5135	0.0206
20	6.1416	0.1628	8.8124	54.1223	0.0185
21	6.7251	0.1487	8.9611	60.2639	0.0166
22	7.3639	0.1358	9.0969	66.9889	0.0149
23	8.0635	0.1240	9.2209	74.3529	0.0134
24	8.8296	0.1133	9.3341	82.4164	0.0121
25	9.6684	0.1034	9.4376	91.2460	0.0110
26	10.5869	0.0945	9.5320	100.9143	0.0099
27	11.5926	0.0863	9.6183	111.5012	0.0090
28	12.6939	0.0788	9.6971	123.0938	0.0081
29	13.8998	0.0719	9.7690	135.7877	0.0074
30	15.2203	0.0657	9.8347	149.6876	0.0067
31	16.6663	0.0600	9.8947	164.9079	0.0061
32	18.2495	0.0548	9.9495	181.5741	0.0055
33	19.9833	0.0500	9.9996	199.8237	0.0050
34	21.8817	0.0457	10.0453	219.8069	0.0045
35	23.9604	0.0417	10.0870	241.6886	0.0041
36	26.2367	0.0381	10.1251	265.6490	0.0038
37	28.7291	0.0348	10.1599	291.8857	0.0034
38	31.4584	0.0318	10.1917	320.6148	0.0031
39	34.4470	0.0290	10.2207	352.0732	0.0028
40	37.7194	0.0265	10.2472	386.5202	0.0026
41	41.3028	0.0242	10.2715	424.2396	0.0024
42	45.2265	0.0221	10.2936	465.5424	0.0021
43	49.5231	0.0202	10.3138	510.7689	0.0020
44	54.2277	0.0184	10.3322	560.2920	0.0018
45	59.3794	0.0168	10.3490	614.5197	0.0016
46	65.0204	0.0154	10.3644	673.8991	0.0015
47	71.1974	0.0140	10.3785	738.9195	0.0014
48	77.9611	0.0128	10.3913	810.1168	0.0012
49	85.3674	0.0117	10.4030	888.0779	0.0011
50	93.4773	0.0107	10.4137	973.4453	0.0010

10%

PERIOD	COMPOUND INTEREST	PRESENT VALUE	PRESENT VALUE OF ANNUITY	AMOUNT OF ANNUITY	SINKING FUND
1	1.1000	0.9091	0.9091	1.0000	1.0000
2	1.2100	0.8264	1.7355	2.1000	0.4762
3	1.3310	0.7513	2.4869	3.3100	0.3021
4	1.4641	0.6830	3.1699	4.6410	0.2155
5	1.6105	0.6209	3.7908	6.1051	0.1638
6	1.7716	0.5645	4.3553	7.7156	0.1296
7	1.9487	0.5132	4.8684	9.4872	0.1054
8	2.1436	0.4665	5.3349	11.4359	0.0874
9	2.3579	0.4241	5.7590	13.5795	0.0736
10	2.5937	0.3855	6.1446	15.9374	0.0627
11	2.8531	0.3505	6.4951	18.5312	0.0540
12	3.1384	0.3186	6.8137	21.3843	0.0468
13	3.4523	0.2897	7.1034	24.5227	0.0408
14	3.7975	0.2633	7.3667	27.9750	0.0357
15	4.1772	0.2394	7.6061	31.7725	0.0315
16	4.5950	0.2176	7.8237	35.9497	0.0278
17	5.0545	0.1978	8.0216	40.5447	0.0247
18	5.5599	0.1799	8.2014	45.5992	0.0219
19	6.1159	0.1635	8.3649	51.1591	0.0195
20	6.7275	0.1486	8.5136	57.2750	0.0175
21	7.4002	0.1351	8.6487	64.0025	0.0156
22	8.1403	0.1228	8.7715	71.4028	0.0140
23	8.9543	0.1117	8.8832	79.5430	0.0126
24	9.8497	0.1015	8.9847	88.4974	0.0113
25	10.8347	0.0923	9.0770	98.3471	0.0102
26	11.9182	0.0839	9.1609	109.1818	0.0092
27	13.1100	0.0763	9.2372	121.1000	0.0083
28	14.4210	0.0693	9.3066	134.2100	0.0075
29	15.8631	0.0630	9.3696	148.6310	0.0067
30	17.4494	0.0573	9.4269	164.4941	0.0061
31	19.1944	0.0521	9.4790	181.9435	0.0055
32	21.1138	0.0474	9.5264	201.1379	0.0050
33	23.2252	0.0431	9.5694	222.2517	0.0045
34	25.5477	0.0391	9.6086	245.4768	0.0041
35	28.1025	0.0356	9.6442	271.0245	0.0037
36	30.9127	0.0323	9.6765	299.1270	0.0033
37	34.0040	0.0294	9.7059	330.0397	0.0030
38	37.4044	0.0267	9.7327	364.0436	0.0027
39	41.1448	0.0243	9.7570	401.4480	0.0025
40	45.2593	0.0221	9.7790	442.5928	0.0023
41	49.7852	0.0201	9.7991	487.8520	0.0020
42	54.7637	0.0183	9.8174	537.6373	0.0019
43	60.2401	0.0166	9.8340	592.4010	0.0017
44	66.2641	0.0151	9.8491	652.6411	0.0015
45	72.8905	0.0137	9.8628	718.9052	0.0014
46	80.1796	0.0125	9.8753	791.7957	0.0013
47	88.1975	0.0113	9.8866	871.9753	0.0011
48	97.0173	0.0103	9.8969	960.1730	0.0010
49	106.7190	0.0094	9.9063	1057.1900	0.0009
50	117.3909	0.0085	9.9148	1163.9090	0.0009

PERIOD	COMPOUND INTEREST	PRESENT VALUE	PRESENT VALUE OF ANNUITY	AMOUNT OF ANNUITY	SINKING FUND
1	1.1050	0.9050	0.9050	1.0000	1.0000
2	1.2210	0.8190	1.7240	2.1050	0.4751
3	1.3492	0.7412	2.4651	3.3260	0.3007
4	1.4909	0.6707	3.1359	4.6753	0.2139
5	1.6474	0.6070	3.7429	6.1662	0.1622
6	1.8204	0.5493	4.2922	7.8136	0.1280
7	2.0116	0.4971	4.7893	9.6340	0.1038
8	2.2228	0.4499	5.2392	11.6456	0.0859
9	2.4562	0.4071	5.6463	13.8684	0.0721
10	2.7141	0.3684	6.0148	16.3246	0.0613
11	2.9991	0.3334	6.3482	19.0387	0.0525
12	3.3140	0.3018	6.6500	22.0377	0.0454
13	3.6619	0.2731	6.9230	25.3517	0.0394
14	4.0464	0.2471	7.1702	29.0136	0.0345
15	4.4713	0.2236	7.3938	33.0600	0.0302
16	4.9408	0.2024	7.5962	37.5313	0.0266
17	5.4596	0.1832	7.7794	42.4721	0.0235
18	6.0328	0.1658	7.9451	47.9317	0.0209
19	6.6663	0.1500	8.0952	53.9645	0.0185
20	7.3662	0.1358	8.2309	60.6308	0.0165
21	8.1397	0.1229	8.3538	67.9970	0.0147
22	8.9944	0.1112	8.4649	76.1367	0.0131
23	9.9388	0.1006	8.5656	85.1311	0.0117
24	10.9823	0.0911	8.6566	95.0699	0.0105
25	12.1355	0.0824	8.7390	106.0522	0.0094
26	13.4097	0.0746	8.8136	118.1877	0.0085
27	14.8177	0.0675	8.8811	131.5974	0.0076
28	16.3736	0.0611	8.9422	146.4151	0.0068
29	18.0928	0.0553	8.9974	162.7887	0.0061
30	19.9926	0.0500	9.0474	180.8815	0.0055
31	22.0918	0.0453	9.0927	200.8741	0.0050
32	24.4114	0.0410	9.1337	222.9659	0.0045
33	26.9746	0.0371	9.1707	247.3773	0.0040
34	29.8070	0.0335	9.2043	274.3519	0.0036
35	32.9367	0.0304	9.2347	304.1588	0.0033
36	36.3950	0.0275	9.2621	337.0955	0.0030
37	40.2165	0.0249	9.2870	373.4906	0.0027
38	44.4392	0.0225	9.3095	413.7070	0.0024
39	49.1054	0.0204	9.3299	458.1463	0.0022
40	54.2614	0.0184	9.3483	507.2517	0.0020
41	59.9589	0.0167	9.3650	561.5131	0.0018
42	66.2546	0.0151	9.3801	621.4720	0.0016
43	73.2113	0.0137	9.3937	687.7266	0.0015
44	80.8985	0.0124	9.4061	760.9378	0.0013
45	89.3928	0.0112	9.4173	841.8363	0.0012
46	98.7791	0.0101	9.4274	931.2291	0.0011
47	109.1509	0.0092	9.4366	1030.0080	0.0010
48	120.6117	0.0083	9.4448	1139.1590	0.0009
49	133.2759	0.0075	9.4523	1259.7710	0.0008
50	147.2699	0.0068	9.4591	1393.0470	0.0007

11%

PERIOD	COMPOUND INTEREST	PRESENT VALUE	PRESENT VALUE OF ANNUITY	AMOUNT OF ANNUITY	SINKING FUND
1	1.1100	0.9009	0.9009	1.0000	1.0000
2	1.2321	0.8116	1.7125	2.1100	0.4739
3	1.3676	0.7312	2.4437	3.3421	0.2992
4	1.5181	0.6587	3.1024	4.7097	0.2123
5	1.6851	0.5935	3.6959	6.2278	0.1606
6	1.8704	0.5346	4.2305	7.9129	0.1264
7	2.0762	0.4817	4.7122	9.7833	0.1022
8	2.3045	0.4339	5.1461	11.8594	0.0843
9	2.5580	0.3909	5.5370	14.1640	0.0706
10	2.8394	0.3522	5.8892	16.7220	0.0598
11	3.1518	0.3173	6.2065	19.5614	0.0511
12	3.4985	0.2858	6.4924	22.7132	0.0440
13	3.8833	0.2575	6.7499	26.2116	0.0382
14	4.3104	0.2320	6.9819	30.0949	0.0332
15	4.7846	0.2090	7.1909	34.4054	0.0291
16	5.3109	0.1883	7.3792	39.1899	0.0255
17	5.8951	0.1696	7.5488	44.5008	0.0225
18	6.5436	0.1528	7.7016	50.3959	0.0198
19	7.2633	0.1377	7.8393	56.9395	0.0176
20	8.0623	0.1240	7.9633	64.2028	0.0156
21	8.9492	0.1117	8.0751	72.2651	0.0138
22	9.9336	0.1007	8.1757	81.2143	0.0123
23	11.0263	0.0907	8.2664	91.1479	0.0110
24	12.2392	0.0817	8.3481	102.1741	0.0098
25	13.5855	0.0736	8.4217	114.4133	0.0087
26	15.0799	0.0663	8.4881	127.9988	0.0078
27	16.7386	0.0597	8.5478	143.0786	0.0070
28	18.5799	0.0538	8.6016	159.8173	0.0063
29	20.6237	0.0485	8.6501	178.3972	0.0056
30	22.8923	0.0437	8.6938	199.0209	0.0050
31	25.4105	0.0394	8.7331	221.9132	0.0045
32	28.2056	0.0355	8.7686	247.3236	0.0040
33	31.3082	0.0319	8.8005	275.5292	0.0036
34	34.7521	0.0288	8.8293	306.8374	0.0033
35	38.5749	0.0259	8.8552	341.5895	0.0029
36	42.8181	0.0234	8.8786	380.1644	0.0026
37	47.5281	0.0210	8.8996	422.9825	0.0024
38	52.7562	0.0190	8.9186	470.5106	0.0021
39	58.5593	0.0171	8.9357	523.2667	0.0019
40	65.0009	0.0154	8.9511	581.8260	0.0017
41	72.1510	0.0139	8.9649	646.8269	0.0015
42	80.0876	0.0125	8.9774	718.9779	0.0014
43	88.8972	0.0112	8.9886	799.0655	0.0013
44	98.6759	0.0101	8.9988	887.9626	0.0011
45	109.5303	0.0091	9.0079	986.6385	0.0010
46	121.5786	0.0082	9.0161	1096.1690	0.0009
47	134.9522	0.0074	9.0235	1217.7470	0.0008
48	149.7970	0.0067	9.0302	1352.7000	0.0007
49	166.2746	0.0060	9.0362	1502.4970	0.0007
50	184.5649	0.0054	9.0417	1668.7710	0.0006

PERIOD	COMPOUND INTEREST	PRESENT VALUE	PRESENT VALUE OF ANNUITY	AMOUNT OF ANNUITY	SINKING FUND
1	1.1150	0.8969	0.8969	1.0000	1.0000
2	1.2432	0.8044	1.7012	2.1150	0.4728
3	1.3862	0.7214	2.4226	3.3582	0.2978
4	1.5456	0.6470	3.0696	4.7444	0.2108
5	1.7234	0.5803	3.6499	6.2900	0.1590
6	1.9215	0.5204	4.1703	8.0134	0.1248
7	2.1425	0.4667	4.6370	9.9349	0.1007
8	2.3889	0.4186	5.0556	12.0774	0.0828
9	2.6636	0.3754	5.4311	14.4663	0.0691
10	2.9699	0.3367	5.7678	17.1300	0.0584
11	3.3115	0.3020	6.0697	20.0999	0.0498
12	3.6923	0.2708	6.3406	23.4114	0.0427
13	4.1169	0.2429	6.5835	27.1037	0.0369
14	4.5904	0.2178	6.8013	31.2206	0.0320
15	5.1183	0.1954	6.9967	35.8110	0.0279
16	5.7069	0.1752	7.1719	40.9293	0.0244
17	6.3632	0.1572	7.3291	46.6361	0.0214
18	7.0949	0.1409	7.4700	52.9993	0.0189
19	7.9108	0.1264	7.5964	60.0942	0.0166
20	8.8206	0.1134	7.7098	68.0050	0.0147
21	9.8349	0.1017	7.8115	76.8256	0.0130
22	10.9660	0.0912	7.9027	86.6606	0.0115
23	12.2271	0.0818	7.9845	97.6265	0.0102
24	13.6332	0.0734	8.0578	109.8536	0.0091
25	15.2010	0.0658	8.1236	123.4867	0.0081
26	16.9491	0.0590	8.1826	138.6877	0.0072
27	18.8982	0.0529	8.2355	155.6368	0.0064
28	21.0715	0.0475	8.2830	174.5350	0.0057
29	23.4948	0.0426	8.3255	195.6066	0.0051
30	26.1967	0.0382	8.3637	219.1013	0.0046
31	29.2093	0.0342	8.3979	245.2980	0.0041
32	32.5683	0.0307	8.4287	274.5072	0.0036
33	36.3137	0.0275	8.4562	307.0755	0.0033
34	40.4898	0.0247	8.4809	343.3892	0.0029
35	45.1461	0.0222	8.5030	383.8790	0.0026
36	50.3379	0.0199	8.5229	429.0250	0.0023
37	56.1267	0.0178	8.5407	479.3629	0.0021
38	62.5813	0.0160	8.5567	535.4896	0.0019
39	69.7782	0.0143	8.5710	598.0710	0.0017
40	77.8027	0.0129	8.5839	667.8491	0.0015
41	86.7500	0.0115	8.5954	745.6517	0.0013
42	96.7262	0.0103	8.6058	832.4017	0.0012
43	107.8497	0.0093	8.6150	929.1278	0.0011
44	120.2524	0.0083	8.6233	1036.9770	0.0010
45	134.0815	0.0075	8.6308	1157.2300	0.0009
46	149.5008	0.0067	8.6375	1291.3110	0.0008
47	166.6934	0.0060	8.6435	1440.8120	0.0007
48	185.8632	0.0054	8.6489	1607.5050	0.0006
49	207.2374	0.0048	8.6537	1793.3690	0.0006
50	231.0697	0.0043	8.6580	2000.6060	0.0005

12%

PERIOD	COMPOUND INTEREST	PRESENT VALUE	PRESENT VALUE OF ANNUITY	AMOUNT OF ANNUITY	SINKING FUND
1	1.1200	0.8929	0.8929	1.0000	1.0000
2	1.2544	0.7972	1.6901	2.1200	0.4717
3	1.4049	0.7118	2.4018	3.3744	0.2963
4	1.5735	0.6355	3.0373	4.7793	0.2092
5	1.7623	0.5674	3.6048	6.3528	0.1574
6	1.9738	0.5066	4.1114	8.1152	0.1232
7	2.2107	0.4523	4.5638	10.0890	0.0991
8	2.4760	0.4039	4.9676	12.2997	0.0813
9	2.7731	0.3606	5.3282	14.7757	0.0677
10	3.1058	0.3220	5.6502	17.5487	0.0570
11	3.4785	0.2875	5.9377	20.6546	0.0484
12	3.8960	0.2567	6.1944	24.1331	0.0414
13	4.3635	0.2292	6.4235	28.0291	0.0357
14	4.8871	0.2046	6.6282	32.3926	0.0309
15	5.4736	0.1827	6.8109	37.2797	0.0268
16	6.1304	0.1631	6.9740	42.7533	0.0234
17	6.8660	0.1456	7.1196	48.8837	0.0205
18	7.6900	0.1300	7.2497	55.7497	0.0179
19	8.6128	0.1161	7.3658	63.4397	0.0158
20	9.6463	0.1037	7.4694	72.0524	0.0139
21	10.8038	0.0926	7.5620	81.6987	0.0122
22	12.1003	0.0826	7.6446	92.5026	0.0108
23	13.5523	0.0738	7.7184	104.6029	0.0096
24	15.1786	0.0659	7.7843	118.1552	0.0085
25	17.0001	0.0588	7.8431	133.3338	0.0075
26	19.0401	0.0525	7.8957	150.3339	0.0067
27	21.3249	0.0469	7.9426	169.3740	0.0059
28	23.8839	0.0419	7.9844	190.6989	0.0052
29	26.7499	0.0374	8.0218	214.5827	0.0047
30	29.9599	0.0334	8.0552	241.3327	0.0041
31	33.5551	0.0298	8.0850	271.2926	0.0037
32	37.5817	0.0266	8.1116	304.8477	0.0033
33	42.0915	0.0238	8.1354	342.4294	0.0029
34	47.1425	0.0212	8.1566	384.5209	0.0026
35	52.7996	0.0189	8.1755	431.6634	0.0023
36	59.1356	0.0169	8.1924	484.4631	0.0021
37	66.2318	0.0151	8.2075	543.5986	0.0018
38	74.1797	0.0135	8.2210	609.8305	0.0016
39	83.0812	0.0120	8.2330	684.0101	0.0015
40	93.0510	0.0107	8.2438	767.0913	0.0013
41	104.2171	0.0096	8.2534	860.1422	0.0012
42	116.7231	0.0086	8.2619	964.3592	0.0010
43	130.7299	0.0076	8.2696	1081.0820	0.0009
44	146.4175	0.0068	8.2764	1211.8120	0.0008
45	163.9876	0.0061	8.2825	1358.2300	0.0007
46	183.6661	0.0054	8.2880	1522.2170	0.0007
47	205.7060	0.0049	8.2928	1705.8830	0.0006
48	230.3908	0.0043	8.2972	1911.5890	0.0005
49	258.0377	0.0039	8.3010	2141.9800	0.0005
50	289.0022	0.0035	8.3045	2400.0180	0.0004

PERIOD	COMPOUND INTEREST	PRESENT VALUE	PRESENT VALUE OF ANNUITY	AMOUNT OF ANNUITY	SINKING FUND
1	1.1250	0.8889	0.8889	1.0000	1.0000
2	1.2656	0.7901	1.6790	2.1250	0.4706
3	1.4238	0.7023	2.3813	3.3906	0.2949
4	1.6018	0.6243	3.0056	4.8145	0.2077
5	1.8020	0.5549	3.5606	6.4163	0.1559
6	2.0273	0.4933	4.0538	8.2183	0.1217
7	2.2807	0.4385	4.4923	10.2456	0.0976
8	2.5658	0.3897	4.8820	12.5263	0.0798
9	2.8865	0.3464	5.2285	15.0921	0.0663
10	3.2473	0.3079	5.5364	17.9786	0.0556
11	3.6532	0.2737	5.8102	21.2259	0.0471
12	4.1099	0.2433	6.0535	24.8791	0.0402
13	4.6236	0.2163	6.2698	28.9890	0.0345
14	5.2016	0.1922	6.4620	33.6126	0.0298
15	5.8518	0.1709	6.6329	38.8142	0.0258
16	6.5833	0.1519	6.7848	44.6660	0.0224
17	7.4062	0.1350	6.9198	51.2492	0.0195
18	8.3319	0.1200	7.0398	58.6554	0.0170
19	9.3734	0.1067	7.1465	66.9873	0.0149
20	10.5451	0.0948	7.2414	76.3607	0.0131
21	11.8632	0.0843	7.3256	86.9058	0.0115
22	13.3461	0.0749	7.4006	98.7691	0.0101
23	15.0144	0.0666	7.4672	112.1152	0.0089
24	16.8912	0.0592	7.5264	127.1296	0.0079
25	19.0026	0.0526	7.5790	144.0208	0.0069
26	21.3779	0.0468	7.6258	163.0234	0.0061
27	24.0502	0.0416	7.6674	184.4013	0.0054
28	27.0564	0.0370	7.7043	208.4515	0.0048
29	30.4385	0.0329	7.7372	235.5079	0.0042
30	34.2433	0.0292	7.7664	265.9464	0.0038
31	38.5237	0.0260	7.7923	300.1897	0.0033
32	43.3392	0.0231	7.8154	338.7134	0.0030
33	48.7566	0.0205	7.8359	382.0526	0.0026
34	54.8512	0.0182	7.8542	430.8092	0.0023
35	61.7075	0.0162	7.8704	485.6603	0.0021
36	69.4210	0.0144	7.8848	547.3679	0.0018
37	78.0986	0.0128	7.8976	616.7888	0.0016
38	87.8609	0.0114	7.9089	694.8874	0.0014
39	98.8436	0.0101	7.9191	782.7483	0.0013
40	111.1990	0.0090	7.9281	881.5918	0.0011
41	125.0989	0.0080	7.9360	992.7908	0.0010
42	140.7362	0.0071	7.9432	1117.8900	0.0009
43	158.3283	0.0063	7.9495	1258.6260	0.0008
44	178.1193	0.0056	7.9551	1416.9540	0.0007
45	200.3842	0.0050	7.9601	1595.0730	0.0006
46	225.4322	0.0044	7.9645	1795.4580	0.0006
47	253.6113	0.0039	7.9685	2020.8900	0.0005
48	285.3127	0.0035	7.9720	2274.5010	0.0004
49	320.9768	0.0031	7.9751	2559.8140	0.0004
50	361.0988	0.0028	7.9778	2880.7900	0.0003

13%

PERIOD	COMPOUND INTEREST	PRESENT VALUE	PRESENT VALUE OF ANNUITY	AMOUNT OF ANNUITY	SINKING FUND
1	1.1300	0.8850	0.8850	1.0000	1.0000
2	1.2769	0.7831	1.6681	2.1300	0.4695
3	1.4429	0.6931	2.3612	3.4069	0.2935
4	1.6305	0.6133	2.9745	4.8498	0.2062
5	1.8424	0.5428	3.5172	6.4803	0.1543
6	2.0820	0.4803	3.9975	8.3227	0.1202
7	2.3526	0.4251	4.4226	10.4047	0.0961
8	2.6584	0.3762	4.7988	12.7573	0.0784
9	3.0040	0.3329	5.1317	15.4157	0.0649
10	3.3946	0.2946	5.4262	18.4197	0.0543
11	3.8359	0.2607	5.6869	21.8143	0.0458
12	4.3345	0.2307	5.9176	25.6502	0.0390
13	4.8980	0.2042	6.1218	29.9847	0.0334
14	5.5348	0.1807	6.3025	34.8827	0.0287
15	6.2543	0.1599	6.4624	40.4174	0.0247
16	7.0673	0.1415	6.6039	46.6717	0.0214
17	7.9861	0.1252	6.7291	53.7390	0.0186
18	9.0243	0.1108	6.8399	61.7251	0.0162
19	10.1974	0.0981	6.9380	70.7494	0.0141
20	11.5231	0.0868	7.0248	80.9468	0.0124
21	13.0211	0.0768	7.1015	92.4698	0.0108
22	14.7138	0.0680	7.1695	105.4909	0.0095
23	16.6266	0.0601	7.2297	120.2047	0.0083
24	18.7881	0.0532	7.2829	136.8313	0.0073
25	21.2305	0.0471	7.3300	155.6194	0.0064
26	23.9905	0.0417	7.3717	176.8499	0.0057
27	27.1093	0.0369	7.4086	200.8404	0.0050
28	30.6335	0.0326	7.4412	227.9497	0.0044
29	34.6158	0.0289	7.4701	258.5831	0.0039
30	39.1159	0.0256	7.4957	293.1989	0.0034
31	44.2009	0.0226	7.5183	332.3148	0.0030
32	49.9470	0.0200	7.5383	376.5156	0.0027
33	56.4402	0.0177	7.5560	426.4627	0.0023
34	63.7774	0.0157	7.5717	482.9028	0.0021
35	72.0684	0.0139	7.5856	546.6802	0.0018
36	81.4373	0.0123	7.5979	618.7486	0.0016
37	92.0242	0.0109	7.6087	700.1858	0.0014
38	103.9873	0.0096	7.6183	792.2100	0.0013
39	117.5057	0.0085	7.6268	896.1972	0.0011
40	132.7814	0.0075	7.6344	1013.7030	0.0010
41	150.0430	0.0067	7.6410	1146.4840	0.0009
42	169.5485	0.0059	7.6469	1296.5270	0.0008
43	191.5899	0.0052	7.6522	1466.0760	0.0007
44	216.4965	0.0046	7.6568	1657.6650	0.0006
45	244.6410	0.0041	7.6609	1874.1620	0.0005
46	276.4444	0.0036	7.6645	2118.8030	0.0005
47	312.3822	0.0032	7.6677	2395.2470	0.0004
48	352.9918	0.0028	7.6705	2707.6290	0.0004
49	398.8807	0.0025	7.6730	3060.6210	0.0003
50	450.7352	0.0022	7.6752	3459.5010	0.0003

PERIOD	COMPOUND INTEREST	PRESENT VALUE	PRESENT VALUE OF ANNUITY	AMOUNT OF ANNUITY	SINKING FUND
1	1.1350	0.8811	0.8811	1.0000	1.0000
2	1.2882	0.7763	1.6573	2.1350	0.4684
3	1.4621	0.6839	2.3413	3.4232	0.2921
4	1.6595	0.6026	2.9438	4.8854	0.2047
5	1.8836	0.5309	3.4747	6.5449	0.1528
6	2.1378	0.4678	3.9425	8.4284	0.1186
7	2.4264	0.4121	4.3546	10.5663	0.0946
8	2.7540	0.3631	4.7177	12.9927	0.0770
9	3.1258	0.3199	5.0377	15.7467	0.0635
10	3.5478	0.2819	5.3195	18.8726	0.0530
11	4.0267	0.2483	5.5679	22.4204	0.0446
12	4.5704	0.2188	5.7867	26.4471	0.0378
13	5.1874	0.1928	5.9794	31.0175	0.0322
14	5.8876	0.1698	6.1493	36.2048	0.0276
15	6.6825	0.1496	6.2989	42.0925	0.0238
16	7.5846	0.1318	6.4308	48.7749	0.0205
17	8.6085	0.1162	6.5469	56.3596	0.0177
18	9.7707	0.1023	6.6493	64.9681	0.0154
19	11.0897	0.0902	6.7395	74.7388	0.0134
20	12.5868	0.0794	6.8189	85.8285	0.0117
21	14.2861	0.0700	6.8889	98.4154	0.0102
22	16.2147	0.0617	6.9506	112.7014	0.0089
23	18.4037	0.0543	7.0049	128.9161	0.0078
24	20.8882	0.0479	7.0528	147.3198	0.0068
25	23.7081	0.0422	7.0950	168.2080	0.0059
26	26.9087	0.0372	7.1321	191.9160	0.0052
27	30.5413	0.0327	7.1649	218.8247	0.0046
28	34.6644	0.0288	7.1937	249.3660	0.0040
29	39.3441	0.0254	7.2191	284.0304	0.0035
30	44.6556	0.0224	7.2415	323.3745	0.0031
31	50.6841	0.0197	7.2613	368.0301	0.0027
32	57.5264	0.0174	7.2786	418.7141	0.0024
33	65.2925	0.0153	7.2940	476.2405	0.0021
34	74.1070	0.0135	7.3075	541.5330	0.0018
35	84.1114	0.0119	7.3193	615.6400	0.0016
36	95.4664	0.0105	7.3298	699.7513	0.0014
37	108.3544	0.0092	7.3390	795.2177	0.0013
38	122.9822	0.0081	7.3472	903.5720	0.0011
39	139.5848	0.0072	7.3543	1026.5540	0.0010
40	158.4288	0.0063	7.3607	1166.1390	0.0009
41	179.8167	0.0056	7.3662	1324.5680	0.0008
42	204.0919	0.0049	7.3711	1504.3840	0.0007
43	231.6443	0.0043	7.3754	1708.4760	0.0006
44	262.9163	0.0038	7.3792	1940.1210	0.0005
45	298.4100	0.0034	7.3826	2203.0370	0.0005
46	338.6953	0.0030	7.3855	2501.4470	0.0004
47	384.4192	0.0026	7.3881	2840.1420	0.0004
48	436.3158	0.0023	7.3904	3224.5610	0.0003
49	495.2184	0.0020	7.3924	3660.8770	0.0003
50	562.0728	0.0018	7.3942	4156.0950	0.0002

14%

PERIOD	COMPOUND INTEREST	PRESENT VALUE	PRESENT VALUE OF ANNUITY	AMOUNT OF ANNUITY	SINKING FUND
1	1.1400	0.8772	0.8772	1.0000	1.0000
2	1.2996	0.7695	1.6467	2.1400	0.4673
3	1.4815	0.6750	2.3216	3.4396	0.2907
4	1.6890	0.5921	2.9137	4.9211	0.2032
5	1.9254	0.5194	3.4331	6.6101	0.1513
6	2.1950	0.4556	3.8887	8.5355	0.1172
7	2.5023	0.3996	4.2883	10.7305	0.0932
8	2.8526	0.3506	4.6389	13.2328	0.0756
9	3.2519	0.3075	4.9464	16.0853	0.0622
10	3.7072	0.2697	5.2161	19.3373	0.0517
11	4.2262	0.2366	5.4527	23.0445	0.0434
12	4.8179	0.2076	5.6603	27.2708	0.0367
13	5.4924	0.1821	5.8424	32.0887	0.0312
14	6.2613	0.1597	6.0021	37.5811	0.0266
15	7.1379	0.1401	6.1422	43.8424	0.0228
16	8.1373	0.1229	6.2651	50.9804	0.0196
17	9.2765	0.1078	6.3729	59.1176	0.0169
18	10.5752	0.0946	6.4674	68.3941	0.0146
19	12.0557	0.0829	6.5504	78.9692	0.0127
20	13.7435	0.0728	6.6231	91.0249	0.0110
21	15.6676	0.0638	6.6870	104.7684	0.0095
22	17.8610	0.0560	6.7429	120.4360	0.0083
23	20.3616	0.0491	6.7921	138.2971	0.0072
24	23.2122	0.0431	6.8351	158.6587	0.0063
25	26.4619	0.0378	6.8729	181.8708	0.0055
26	30.1666	0.0331	6.9061	208.3328	0.0048
27	34.3899	0.0291	6.9352	238.4994	0.0042
28	39.2045	0.0255	6.9607	272.8893	0.0037
29	44.6931	0.0224	6.9830	312.0938	0.0032
30	50.9502	0.0196	7.0027	356.7869	0.0028
31	58.0832	0.0172	7.0199	407.7371	0.0025
32	66.2148	0.0151	7.0350	465.8203	0.0021
33	75.4849	0.0132	7.0482	532.0351	0.0019
34	86.0528	0.0116	7.0599	607.5200	0.0016
35	98.1002	0.0102	7.0700	693.5728	0.0014
36	111.8342	0.0089	7.0790	791.6730	0.0013
37	127.4910	0.0078	7.0868	903.5072	0.0011
38	145.3398	0.0069	7.0937	1030.9980	0.0010
39	165.6873	0.0060	7.0997	1176.3380	0.0009
40	188.8836	0.0053	7.1050	1342.0250	0.0007
41	215.3273	0.0046	7.1097	1530.9090	0.0007
42	245.4731	0.0041	7.1138	1746.2360	0.0006
43	279.8393	0.0036	7.1173	1991.7090	0.0005
44	319.0168	0.0031	7.1205	2271.5480	0.0004
45	363.6792	0.0027	7.1232	2590.5650	0.0004
46	414.5943	0.0024	7.1256	2954.2450	0.0003
47	472.6374	0.0021	7.1277	3368.8390	0.0003
48	538.8066	0.0019	7.1296	3841.4760	0.0003
49	614.2396	0.0016	7.1312	4380.2830	0.0002
50	700.2331	0.0014	7.1327	4994.5230	0.0002

PERIOD	COMPOUND INTEREST	PRESENT VALUE	PRESENT VALUE OF ANNUITY	AMOUNT OF ANNUITY	SINKING FUND
1	1.1450	0.8734	0.8734	1.0000	1.0000
2	1.3110	0.7628	1.6361	2.1450	0.4662
3	1.5011	0.6662	2.3023	3.4560	0.2893
4	1.7188	0.5818	2.8841	4.9571	0.2017
5	1.9680	0.5081	3.3922	6.6759	0.1498
6	2.2534	0.4438	3.8360	8.6439	0.1157
7	2.5801	0.3876	4.2236	10.8973	0.0918
8	2.9542	0.3385	4.5621	13.4774	0.0742
9	3.3826	0.2956	4.8577	16.4316	0.0609
10	3.8731	0.2582	5.1159	19.8142	0.0505
11	4.4347	0.2255	5.3414	23.6873	0.0422
12	5.0777	0.1969	5.5383	28.1220	0.0356
13	5.8139	0.1720	5.7103	33.1996	0.0301
14	6.6570	0.1502	5.8606	39.0136	0.0256
15	7.6222	0.1312	5.9918	45.6705	0.0219
16	8.7275	0.1146	6.1063	53.2928	0.0188
17	9.9929	0.1001	6.2064	62.0202	0.0161
18	11.4419	0.0874	6.2938	72.0131	0.0139
19	13.1010	0.0763	6.3701	83.4551	0.0120
20	15.0006	0.0667	6.4368	96.5560	0.0104
21	17.1757	0.0582	6.4950	111.5566	0.0090
22	19.6662	0.0508	6.5459	128.7324	0.0078
23	22.5178	0.0444	6.5903	148.3986	0.0067
24	25.7829	0.0388	6.6291	170.9163	0.0059
25	29.5214	0.0339	6.6629	196.6992	0.0051
26	33.8020	0.0296	6.6925	226.2205	0.0044
27	38.7033	0.0258	6.7184	260.0225	0.0038
28	44.3152	0.0226	6.7409	298.7258	0.0033
29	50.7409	0.0197	6.7606	343.0410	0.0029
30	58.0984	0.0172	6.7778	393.7819	0.0025
31	66.5226	0.0150	6.7929	451.8802	0.0022
32	76.1684	0.0131	6.8060	518.4028	0.0019
33	87.2128	0.0115	6.8175	594.5712	0.0017
34	99.8587	0.0100	6.8275	681.7840	0.0015
35	114.3382	0.0087	6.8362	781.6426	0.0013
36	130.9172	0.0076	6.8439	895.9808	0.0011
37	149.9002	0.0067	6.8505	1026.8980	0.0010
38	171.6357	0.0058	6.8564	1176.7980	0.0008
39	196.5229	0.0051	6.8615	1348.4340	0.0007
40	225.0187	0.0044	6.8659	1544.9560	0.0006
41	257.6464	0.0039	6.8698	1769.9750	0.0006
42	295.0051	0.0034	6.8732	2027.6220	0.0005
43	337.7808	0.0030	6.8761	2322.6270	0.0004
44	386.7590	0.0026	6.8787	2660.4070	0.0004
45	442.8391	0.0023	6.8810	3047.1660	0.0003
46	507.0507	0.0020	6.8830	3490.0050	0.0003
47	580.5730	0.0017	6.8847	3997.0550	0.0003
48	664.7561	0.0015	6.8862	4577.6280	0.0002
49	761.1456	0.0013	6.8875	5242.3840	0.0002
50	871.5118	0.0011	6.8886	6003.5300	0.0002

15%

PERIOD	COMPOUND INTEREST	PRESENT VALUE	PRESENT VALUE OF ANNUITY	AMOUNT OF ANNUITY	SINKING FUND
1	1.1500	0.8696	0.8696	1.0000	1.0000
2	1.3225	0.7561	1.6257	2.1500	0.4651
3	1.5209	0.6575	2.2832	3.4725	0.2880
4	1.7490	0.5718	2.8550	4.9934	0.2003
5	2.0114	0.4972	3.3522	6.7424	0.1483
6	2.3131	0.4323	3.7845	8.7537	0.1142
7	2.6600	0.3759	4.1604	11.0668	0.0904
8	3.0590	0.3269	4.4873	13.7268	0.0729
9	3.5179	0.2843	4.7716	16.7858	0.0596
10	4.0456	0.2472	5.0188	20.3037	0.0493
11	4.6524	0.2149	5.2337	24.3493	0.0411
12	5.3503	0.1869	5.4206	29.0017	0.0345
13	6.1528	0.1625	5.5831	34.3519	0.0291
14	7.0757	0.1413	5.7245	40.5047	0.0247
15	8.1371	0.1229	5.8474	47.5804	0.0210
16	9.3576	0.1069	5.9542	55.7175	0.0179
17	10.7613	0.0929	6.0472	65.0751	0.0154
18	12.3755	0.0808	6.1280	75.8364	0.0132
19	14.2318	0.0703	6.1982	88.2118	0.0113
20	16.3665	0.0611	6.2593	102.4436	0.0098
21	18.8215	0.0531	6.3125	118.8101	0.0084
22	21.6447	0.0462	6.3587	137.6317	0.0073
23	24.8915	0.0402	6.3988	159.2764	0.0063
24	28.6252	0.0349	6.4338	184.1679	0.0054
25	32.9190	0.0304	6.4641	212.7930	0.0047
26	37.8568	0.0264	6.4906	245.7120	0.0041
27	43.5353	0.0230	6.5135	283.5688	0.0035
28	50.0656	0.0200	6.5335	327.1041	0.0031
29	57.5755	0.0174	6.5509	377.1697	0.0027
30	66.2118	0.0151	6.5660	434.7452	0.0023
31	76.1436	0.0131	6.5791	500.9570	0.0020
32	87.5651	0.0114	6.5905	577.1005	0.0017
33	100.6998	0.0099	6.6005	664.6656	0.0015
34	115.8048	0.0086	6.6091	765.3654	0.0013
35	133.1755	0.0075	6.6166	881.1702	0.0011
36	153.1519	0.0065	6.6231	1014.3460	0.0010
37	176.1246	0.0057	6.6288	1167.4980	0.0009
38	202.5433	0.0049	6.6338	1343.6220	0.0007
39	232.9248	0.0043	6.6380	1546.1660	0.0006
40	267.8636	0.0037	6.6418	1779.0910	0.0006
41	308.0431	0.0032	6.6450	2046.9540	0.0005
42	354.2496	0.0028	6.6478	2354.9970	0.0004
43	407.3870	0.0025	6.6503	2709.2470	0.0004
44	468.4951	0.0021	6.6524	3116.6340	0.0003
45	538.7693	0.0019	6.6543	3585.1290	0.0003
46	619.5847	0.0016	6.6559	4123.8990	0.0002
47	712.5224	0.0014	6.6573	4743.4830	0.0002
48	819.4008	0.0012	6.6585	5456.0060	0.0002
49	942.3109	0.0011	6.6596	6275.4070	0.0002
50	1083.6580	0.0009	6.6605	7217.7170	0.0001

COMMON FRACTION TO DECIMAL CONVERSIONS

Fraction	Decimal equivalent	Fraction	Decimal equivalent
$\frac{1}{2}$	.50	$\frac{1}{7}$	$.14\frac{2}{7}$ (.143)
$\frac{1}{3}$	$.33\frac{1}{3}$ (.33$\overline{3}$)	$\frac{1}{8}$	$.12\frac{1}{2}$ (.125)
$\frac{2}{3}$	$.66\frac{2}{3}$ (.66$\overline{6}$)	$\frac{3}{8}$	$.37\frac{1}{2}$ (.375)
$\frac{1}{4}$	.25	$\frac{5}{8}$	$.62\frac{1}{2}$ (.625)
$\frac{3}{4}$	.75	$\frac{7}{8}$	$.87\frac{1}{2}$ (.875)
$\frac{1}{5}$	.20	$\frac{1}{9}$	$.11\overline{1}$
$\frac{2}{5}$	.40	$\frac{1}{10}$	.10
$\frac{3}{5}$	.60	$\frac{1}{12}$	$.08\frac{1}{3}$ (.08$\overline{3}$)
$\frac{4}{5}$	.80	$\frac{1}{15}$	$.06\frac{2}{3}$ (.06$\overline{6}$)
$\frac{1}{6}$	$.16\frac{2}{3}$ (.16$\overline{6}$)	$\frac{1}{16}$	$.06\frac{1}{4}$ (.0625)
$\frac{5}{6}$	$.83\frac{1}{3}$ (.83$\overline{3}$)	$\frac{1}{20}$	.05
		$\frac{1}{25}$	.04

MASSACHUSETTS DEPARTMENT OF REVENUE
5% SALES TAX SCHEDULE
INCLUDING MEALS, PREPARED FOOD AND/OR ALCOHOLIC BEVERAGES,

AMOUNT OF SALE	TAX	AMOUNT OF SALE	TAX
$.10 - $.29	$.01	$7.70 - $7.89	$.39
.30 - .49	.02	7.90 - 8.09	.40
.50 - .69	.03	8.10 - 8.29	.41
.70 - .89	.04	8.30 - 8.49	.42
.90 - 1.09	.05	8.50 - 8.69	.43
1.10 - 1.29	.06	8.70 - 8.89	.44
1.30 - 1.49	.07	8.90 - 9.09	.45
1.50 - 1.69	.08	9.10 - 9.29	.46
1.70 - 1.89	.09	9.30 - 9.49	.47
1.90 - 2.09	.10	9.50 - 9.69	.48
2.10 - 2.29	.11	9.70 - 9.89	.49
2.30 - 2.49	.12	9.90 - 10.09	.50
2.50 - 2.69	.13	10.10 - 10.29	.51
2.70 - 2.89	.14	10.30 - 10.49	.52
2.90 - 3.09	.15	10.50 - 10.69	.53
3.10 - 3.29	.16	10.70 - 10.89	.54
3.30 - 3.49	.17	10.90 - 11.09	.55
3.50 - 3.69	.18	11.10 - 11.29	.56
3.70 - 3.89	.19	11.30 - 11.49	.57
3.90 - 4.09	.20	11.50 - 11.69	.58
4.10 - 4.29	.21	11.70 - 11.89	.59
4.30 - 4.49	.22	11.90 - 12.09	.60
4.50 - 4.69	.23	12.10 - 12.29	.61
4.70 - 4.89	.24	12.30 - 12.49	.62
4.90 - 5.09	.25	12.50 - 12.69	.63
5.10 - 5.29	.26	12.70 - 12.89	.64
5.30 - 5.49	.27	12.90 - 13.09	.65
5.50 - 5.69	.28	13.10 - 13.29	.66
5.70 - 5.89	.29	13.30 - 13.49	.67
5.90 - 6.09	.30	13.50 - 13.69	.68
6.10 - 6.29	.31	13.70 - 13.89	.69
6.30 - 6.49	.32	13.90 - 14.09	.70
6.50 - 6.69	.33	14.10 - 14.29	.71
6.70 - 6.89	.34	14.30 - 14.49	.72
6.90 - 7.09	.35	14.50 - 14.69	.73
7.10 - 7.29	.36	14.70 - 14.89	.74
7.30 - 7.49	.37	14.90 - 15.09	.75
7.50 - 7.69	.38	15.10 - 15.29	.76

CONTINUED ON REVERSE →

RC/NH-775

BBC/NH/775B

AMOUNT OF SALE	TAX	AMOUNT OF SALE	TAX
$15.30 - $15.49	$ .77	$22.70 - $22.89	$1.14
15.50 - 15.69	.78	22.90 - 23.09	1.15
15.70 - 15.89	.79	23.10 - 23.29	1.16
15.90 - 16.09	.80	23.30 - 23.49	1.17
16.10 - 16.29	.81	23.50 - 23.69	1.18
16.30 - 16.49	.82	23.70 - 23.89	1.19
16.50 - 16.69	.83	23.90 - 24.09	1.20
16.70 - 16.89	.84	24.10 - 24.29	1.21
16.90 - 17.09	.85	24.30 - 24.49	1.22
17.10 - 17.29	.86	24.50 - 24.69	1.23
17.30 - 17.49	.87	24.70 - 24.89	1.24
17.50 - 17.69	.88	24.90 - 25.09	1.25
17.70 - 17.89	.89	25.10 - 25.29	1.26
17.90 - 18.09	.90	25.30 - 25.49	1.27
18.10 - 18.29	.91	25.50 - 25.69	1.28
18.30 - 18.49	.92	25.70 - 25.89	1.29
18.50 - 18.69	.93	25.90 - 26.09	1.30
18.70 - 18.89	.94	26.10 - 26.29	1.31
18.90 - 19.09	.95	26.30 - 26.49	1.32
19.10 - 19.29	.96	26.50 - 26.69	1.33
19.30 - 19.49	.97	26.70 - 26.89	1.34
19.50 - 19.69	.98	26.90 - 27.09	1.35
19.70 - 19.89	.99	27.10 - 27.29	1.36
19.90 - 20.09	1.00	27.30 - 27.49	1.37
20.10 - 20.29	1.01	27.50 - 27.69	1.38
20.30 - 20.49	1.02	27.70 - 27.89	1.39
20.50 - 20.69	1.03	27.90 - 28.09	1.40
20.70 - 20.89	1.04	28.10 - 28.29	1.41
20.90 - 21.09	1.05	28.30 - 28.49	1.42
21.10 - 21.29	1.06	28.50 - 28.69	1.43
21.30 - 21.49	1.07	28.70 - 28.89	1.44
21.50 - 21.69	1.08	28.90 - 29.09	1.45
21.70 - 21.89	1.09	29.10 - 29.29	1.46
21.90 - 22.09	1.10	29.30 - 29.49	1.47
22.10 - 22.29	1.11	29.50 - 29.69	1.48
22.30 - 22.49	1.12	29.70 - 29.89	1.49
22.50 - 22.69	1.13	29.90 - 30.09	1.50

ON ANY CHARGE OVER $30.09, ADAPT ABOVE AMOUNTS OR MULTIPLY BY .05. THE TAX MUST BE COMPUTED ON THE TOTAL SALE AND NOT ON PRICES OF INDIVIDUAL ITEMS INCLUDED IN THE SALE.

ST-3, 5% Rate   COMMISSIONER OF REVENUE

MARRIED Persons—WEEKLY Payroll Period

If the wages are–		And the number of withholding allowances claimed is—										
At least	But less than	0	1	2	3	4	5	6	7	8	9	10
		The amount of income tax to be withheld is—										
$740	$750	93	86	79	72	64	57	50	43	36	28	21
750	760	95	88	80	73	66	59	52	44	37	30	23
760	770	96	89	82	75	67	60	53	46	39	31	24
770	780	98	91	83	76	69	62	55	47	40	33	26
780	790	99	92	85	78	70	63	56	49	42	34	27
790	800	101	94	86	79	72	65	58	50	43	36	29
800	810	102	95	88	81	73	66	59	52	45	37	30
810	820	104	97	89	82	75	68	61	53	46	39	32
820	830	105	98	91	84	76	69	62	55	48	40	33
830	840	108	100	92	85	78	71	64	56	49	42	35
840	850	111	101	94	87	79	72	65	58	51	43	36
850	860	113	103	95	88	81	74	67	59	52	45	38
860	870	116	104	97	90	82	75	68	61	54	46	39
870	880	119	106	98	91	84	77	70	62	55	48	41
880	890	122	108	100	93	85	78	71	64	57	49	42
890	900	125	111	101	94	87	80	73	65	58	51	44
900	910	127	114	103	96	88	81	74	67	60	52	45
910	920	130	117	104	97	90	83	76	68	61	54	47
920	930	133	119	106	99	91	84	77	70	63	55	48
930	940	136	122	109	100	93	86	79	71	64	57	50
940	950	139	125	112	102	94	87	80	73	66	58	51
950	960	141	128	114	103	96	89	82	74	67	60	53
960	970	144	131	117	105	97	90	83	76	69	61	54
970	980	147	133	120	107	99	92	85	77	70	63	56
980	990	150	136	123	109	100	93	86	79	72	64	57
990	1,000	153	139	126	112	102	95	88	80	73	66	59
1,000	1,010	155	142	128	115	103	96	89	82	75	67	60
1,010	1,020	158	145	131	118	105	98	91	83	76	69	62
1,020	1,030	161	147	134	121	107	99	92	85	78	70	63
1,030	1,040	164	150	137	123	110	101	94	86	79	72	65
1,040	1,050	167	153	140	126	113	102	95	88	81	73	66
1,050	1,060	169	156	142	129	115	104	97	89	82	75	68
1,060	1,070	172	159	145	132	118	105	98	91	84	76	69
1,070	1,080	175	161	148	135	121	108	100	92	85	78	71
1,080	1,090	178	164	151	137	124	110	101	94	87	79	72
1,090	1,100	181	167	154	140	127	113	103	95	88	81	74
1,100	1,110	183	170	156	143	129	116	104	97	90	82	75
1,110	1,120	186	173	159	146	132	119	106	98	91	84	77
1,120	1,130	189	175	162	149	135	122	108	100	93	85	78
1,130	1,140	192	178	165	151	138	124	111	101	94	87	80
1,140	1,150	195	181	168	154	141	127	114	103	96	88	81
1,150	1,160	197	184	170	157	143	130	117	104	97	90	83
1,160	1,170	200	187	173	160	146	133	119	106	99	91	84
1,170	1,180	203	189	176	163	149	136	122	109	100	93	86
1,180	1,190	206	192	179	165	152	138	125	111	102	94	87
1,190	1,200	209	195	182	168	155	141	128	114	103	96	89
1,200	1,210	211	198	184	171	157	144	131	117	105	97	90
1,210	1,220	214	201	187	174	160	147	133	120	106	99	92
1,220	1,230	217	203	190	177	163	150	136	123	109	100	93
1,230	1,240	220	206	193	179	166	152	139	125	112	102	95
1,240	1,250	223	209	196	182	169	155	142	128	115	103	96
1,250	1,260	225	212	198	185	171	158	145	131	118	105	98
1,260	1,270	228	215	201	188	174	161	147	134	120	107	99
1,270	1,280	231	217	204	191	177	164	150	137	123	110	101
1,280	1,290	234	220	207	193	180	166	153	139	126	113	102
1,290	1,300	237	223	210	196	183	169	156	142	129	115	104
1,300	1,310	239	226	212	199	185	172	159	145	132	118	105
1,310	1,320	242	229	215	202	188	175	161	148	134	121	107
1,320	1,330	245	231	218	205	191	178	164	151	137	124	110
1,330	1,340	248	234	221	207	194	180	167	153	140	127	113
1,340	1,350	251	237	224	210	197	183	170	156	143	129	116
1,350	1,360	253	240	226	213	199	186	173	159	146	132	119
1,360	1,370	256	243	229	216	202	189	175	162	148	135	121
1,370	1,380	259	245	232	219	205	192	178	165	151	138	124
1,380	1,390	262	248	235	221	208	194	181	167	154	141	127

SINGLE Persons—MONTHLY Payroll Period

If the wages are—		And the number of withholding allowances claimed is—										
At least	But less than	0	1	2	3	4	5	6	7	8	9	10
		The amount of income tax to be withheld is—										
$2,440	$2,480	388	330	274	243	212	180	149	118	87	55	24
2,480	2,520	399	341	283	249	218	186	155	124	93	61	30
2,520	2,560	411	352	294	255	224	192	161	130	99	67	36
2,560	2,600	422	363	305	261	230	198	167	136	105	73	42
2,600	2,640	433	375	316	267	236	204	173	142	111	79	48
2,640	2,680	444	386	328	273	242	210	179	148	117	85	54
2,680	2,720	455	397	339	280	248	216	185	154	123	91	60
2,720	2,760	467	408	350	292	254	222	191	160	129	97	66
2,760	2,800	478	419	361	303	260	228	197	166	135	103	72
2,800	2,840	489	431	372	314	266	234	203	172	141	109	78
2,840	2,880	500	442	384	325	272	240	209	178	147	115	84
2,880	2,920	511	453	395	336	278	246	215	184	153	121	90
2,920	2,960	523	464	406	348	289	252	221	190	159	127	96
2,960	3,000	534	475	417	359	300	258	227	196	165	133	102
3,000	3,040	545	487	428	370	312	264	233	202	171	139	108
3,040	3,080	556	498	440	381	323	270	239	208	177	145	114
3,080	3,120	567	509	451	392	334	276	245	214	183	151	120
3,120	3,160	579	520	462	404	345	287	251	220	189	157	126
3,160	3,200	590	531	473	415	356	298	257	226	195	163	132
3,200	3,240	601	543	484	426	368	309	263	232	201	169	138
3,240	3,280	612	554	496	437	379	321	269	238	207	175	144
3,280	3,320	623	565	507	448	390	332	275	244	213	181	150
3,320	3,360	635	576	518	460	401	343	285	250	219	187	156
3,360	3,400	646	587	529	471	412	354	296	256	225	193	162
3,400	3,440	657	599	540	482	424	365	307	262	231	199	168
3,440	3,480	668	610	552	493	435	377	318	268	237	205	174
3,480	3,520	679	621	563	504	446	388	329	274	243	211	180
3,520	3,560	691	632	574	516	457	399	341	282	249	217	186
3,560	3,600	702	643	585	527	468	410	352	293	255	223	192
3,600	3,640	713	655	596	538	480	421	363	305	261	229	198
3,640	3,680	724	666	608	549	491	433	374	316	267	235	204
3,680	3,720	735	677	619	560	502	444	385	327	273	241	210
3,720	3,760	747	688	630	572	513	455	397	338	280	247	216
3,760	3,800	758	699	641	583	524	466	408	349	291	253	222
3,800	3,840	769	711	652	594	536	477	419	361	302	259	228
3,840	3,880	780	722	664	605	547	489	430	372	314	265	234
3,880	3,920	791	733	675	616	558	500	441	383	325	271	240
3,920	3,960	803	744	686	628	569	511	453	394	336	278	246
3,960	4,000	814	755	697	639	580	522	464	405	347	289	252
4,000	4,040	825	767	708	650	592	533	475	417	358	300	258
4,040	4,080	836	778	720	661	603	545	486	428	370	311	264
4,080	4,120	847	789	731	672	614	556	497	439	381	322	270
4,120	4,160	859	800	742	684	625	567	509	450	392	334	276
4,160	4,200	870	811	753	695	636	578	520	461	403	345	286
4,200	4,240	881	823	764	706	648	589	531	473	414	356	298
4,240	4,280	892	834	776	717	659	601	542	484	426	367	309
4,280	4,320	903	845	787	728	670	612	553	495	437	378	320
4,320	4,360	915	856	798	740	681	623	565	506	448	390	331
4,360	4,400	927	867	809	751	692	634	576	517	459	401	342
4,400	4,440	940	879	820	762	704	645	587	529	470	412	354
4,440	4,480	952	890	832	773	715	657	598	540	482	423	365
4,480	4,520	965	901	843	784	726	668	609	551	493	434	376
4,520	4,560	977	912	854	796	737	679	621	562	504	446	387
4,560	4,600	989	925	865	807	748	690	632	573	515	457	398
4,600	4,640	1,002	937	876	818	760	701	643	585	526	468	410
4,640	4,680	1,014	950	888	829	771	713	654	596	538	479	421
4,680	4,720	1,027	962	899	840	782	724	665	607	549	490	432
4,720	4,760	1,039	974	910	852	793	735	677	618	560	502	443
4,760	4,800	1,051	987	922	863	804	746	688	629	571	513	454
4,800	4,840	1,064	999	935	874	816	757	699	641	582	524	466
4,840	4,880	1,076	1,012	947	885	827	769	710	652	594	535	477
4,880	4,920	1,089	1,024	959	896	838	780	721	663	605	546	488
4,920	4,960	1,101	1,036	972	908	849	791	733	674	616	558	499
4,960	5,000	1,113	1,049	984	920	860	802	744	685	627	569	510
5,000	5,040	1,126	1,061	997	932	872	813	755	697	638	580	522

PERCENTAGE METHOD
INCOME TAX
WITHHOLDING TABLE

Payroll period	One withholding allowance
Weekly	$48.08
Biweekly	96.15
Semimonthly	104.17
Monthly	208.33
Quarterly	625.00
Semiannually	1,250.00
Annually	2,500.00
Daily or miscellaneous (each day of the payroll period)	9.62

Tables for Percentage Method of Withholding

TABLE 1—WEEKLY Payroll Period

(a) SINGLE person (including head of household)—

If the amount of wages (after subtracting withholding allowances) is:		The amount of income tax to withhold is:	
Not over $50		$0	
Over—	But not over—		of excess over—
$50	—$476 . . .	15%	—$50
$476	—$999 . . .	$63.90 plus 28%	—$476
$999	—$2,295 . .	$210.34 plus 31%	—$999
$2,295	—$4,960 . .	$612.10 plus 36%	—$2,295
$4,960		$1,571.50 plus 39.6%	—$4,960

(b) MARRIED person—

If the amount of wages (after subtracting withholding allowances) is:		The amount of income tax to withhold is:	
Not over $123		$0	
Over—	But not over—		of excess over—
$123	—$828 . . .	15%	—$123
$828	—$1,664 . .	$105.75 plus 28%	—$828
$1,664	—$2,839 . .	$339.83 plus 31%	—$1,664
$2,839	—$5,011 . .	$704.08 plus 36%	—$2,839
$5,011		$1,486.00 plus 39.6%	—$5,011

TABLE 2—BIWEEKLY Payroll Period

(a) SINGLE person (including head of household)—

If the amount of wages (after subtracting withholding allowances) is:		The amount of income tax to withhold is:	
Not over $100		$0	
Over—	But not over—		of excess over—
$100	—$952 . . .	15%	—$100
$952	—$1,998 . .	$127.80 plus 28%	—$952
$1,998	—$4,590 . .	$420.68 plus 31%	—$1,998
$4,590	—$9,919 . .	$1,224.20 plus 36%	—$4,590
$9,919		$3,142.64 plus 39.6%	—$9,919

(b) MARRIED person—

If the amount of wages (after subtracting withholding allowances) is:		The amount of income tax to withhold is:	
Not over $246		$0	
Over—	But not over—		of excess over—
$246	—$1,656 . .	15%	—$246
$1,656	—$3,329 . .	$211.50 plus 28%	—$1,656
$3,329	—$5,679 . .	$679.94 plus 31%	—$3,329
$5,679	—$10,021 .	$1,408.44 plus 36%	—$5,679
$10,021		$2,971.56 plus 39.6%	—$10,021

TABLE 3—SEMIMONTHLY Payroll Period

(a) SINGLE person (including head of household)—

If the amount of wages (after subtracting withholding allowances) is:		The amount of income tax to withhold is:	
Not over $108		$0	
Over—	But not over—		of excess over—
$108	—$1,031 . .	15%	—$108
$1,031	—$2,165 . .	$138.45 plus 28%	—$1,031
$2,165	—$4,973 . .	$455.97 plus 31%	—$2,165
$4,973	—$10,746 .	$1,326.45 plus 36%	—$4,973
$10,746		$3,404.73 plus 39.6%	—$10,746

(b) MARRIED person—

If the amount of wages (after subtracting withholding allowances) is:		The amount of income tax to withhold is:	
Not over $267		$0	
Over—	But not over—		of excess over—
$267	—$1,794 . .	15%	—$267
$1,794	—$3,606 . .	$229.05 plus 28%	—$1,794
$3,606	—$6,152 . .	$736.41 plus 31%	—$3,606
$6,152	—$10,856 .	$1,525.67 plus 36%	—$6,152
$10,856		$3,219.11 plus 39.6%	—$10,856

TABLE 4—MONTHLY Payroll Period

(a) SINGLE person (including head of household)—

If the amount of wages (after subtracting withholding allowances) is:		The amount of income tax to withhold is:	
Not over $217		$0	
Over—	But not over—		of excess over—
$217	—$2,063 . .	15%	—$217
$2,063	—$4,329 . .	$276.90 plus 28%	—$2,063
$4,329	—$9,946 . .	$911.38 plus 31%	—$4,329
$9,946	—$21,492 .	$2,652.65 plus 36%	—$9,946
$21,492		$6,809.21 plus 39.6%	—$21,492

(b) MARRIED person—

If the amount of wages (after subtracting withholding allowances) is:		The amount of income tax to withhold is:	
Not over $533		$0	
Over—	But not over—		of excess over—
$533	—$3,588 . .	15%	—$533
$3,588	—$7,213 . .	$458.25 plus 28%	—$3,588
$7,213	—$12,304 .	$1,473.25 plus 31%	—$7,213
$12,304	—$21,713 .	$3,051.46 plus 36%	—$12,304
$21,713		$6,438.70 plus 39.6%	—$21,713

INTEREST ON A $1 DEPOSIT COMPOUNDED DAILY—360-DAY BASIS

Number of years	6.00%	6.50%	7.00%	7.50%	8.00%	8.50%	9.00%	9.50%	10.00%
1	1.0618	1.0672	1.0725	1.0779	1.0833	1.0887	1.0942	1.0996	1.1052
2	1.1275	1.1388	1.1503	1.1618	1.1735	1.1853	1.1972	1.2092	1.2214
3	1.1972	1.2153	1.2337	1.2523	1.2712	1.2904	1.3099	1.3297	1.3498
4	1.2712	1.2969	1.3231	1.3498	1.3771	1.4049	1.4333	1.4622	1.4917
5	1.3498	1.3840	1.4190	1.4549	1.4917	1.5295	1.5682	1.6079	1.6486
6	1.4333	1.4769	1.5219	1.5682	1.6160	1.6652	1.7159	1.7681	1.8220
7	1.5219	1.5761	1.6322	1.6904	1.7506	1.8129	1.8775	1.9443	2.0136
8	1.6160	1.6819	1.7506	1.8220	1.8963	1.9737	2.0543	2.1381	2.2253
9	1.7159	1.7949	1.8775	1.9639	2.0543	2.1488	2.2477	2.3511	2.4593
10	1.8220	1.9154	2.0136	2.1168	2.2253	2.3394	2.4593	2.5854	2.7179
15	2.4594	2.6509	2.8574	3.0799	3.3197	3.5782	3.8568	4.1571	4.4808
20	3.3198	3.6689	4.0546	4.4810	4.9522	5.4728	6.0482	6.6842	7.3870
25	4.4811	5.0777	5.7536	6.5195	7.3874	8.3708	9.4851	10.7477	12.1782
30	6.0487	7.0275	8.1645	9.4855	11.0202	12.8032	14.8747	17.2813	20.0772

REBATE FRACTION TABLE BASED ON RULE OF 78

Months to go	Sum of digits	Months to go	Sum of digits	Months to go	Sum of digits	Months to go	Sum of digits
1	1	16	136	31	496	46	1,081
2	3	17	153	32	528	47	1,128
3	6	18	171	33	561	48	1,176
4	10	19	190	34	595	49	1,225
5	15	20	210	35	630	50	1,275
6	21	21	231	36	666	51	1,326
7	28	22	253	37	703	52	1,378
8	36	23	276	38	741	53	1,431
9	45	24	300	39	780	54	1,485
10	55	25	325	40	820	55	1,540
11	66	26	351	41	861	56	1,596
12	78	27	378	42	903	57	1,653
13	91	28	406	43	946	58	1,711
14	105	29	435	44	990	59	1,770
15	120	30	465	45	1,035	60	1,830

THE TAX REFORM ACT UPDATE: ACCELERATED COST RECOVERY SYSTEM FOR ASSETS PLACED IN SERVICE AFTER DECEMBER 31, 1986*

The following classes use a 200% declining-balance, switching to straight-line:
↓

3-year: Race horses more than two years old or any horse other than a race horse that is more than 12 years old at time placed into service; special tools of certain industries.

5-year: Automobiles (not luxury); taxis; light general-purpose trucks, semiconductor manufacturing equipment; computer-based telephone central office switching equipment; qualified technological equipment; property used in connection with research and experimentation.

7-year: Railroad track; single-purpose agricultural (pigpens) or horticultural structure; fixtures, equipment, and furniture.

10-year: New law doesn't add any specific property under this class.

The following classes use 150% declining-balance, switching to straight-line:
↓

15-year: Municipal wastewater treatment plants; telephone distribution plants and comparable equipment for two-way exchange of voice and data communications.

20-year: Municipal sewers.

The following classes use straight-line:
↓

27.5-year: Only residential rental property.
31.5-year: Only nonresidential real property.

*New tax bill of 1989 requires for cellular phones the straight-line depreciation unless 50% is for business use.

MACRS

Year of recovery	3-year	5-year	7-year	10-year	15-year	20-year
1	33%	20.00%	14.28%	10.00%	5.00%	3.75%
2	45%	32.00%	24.49%	18.00%	9.50%	7.22%
3	15%	19.20%	17.49%	14.40%	8.55%	6.68%
4	7%	11.52%	12.49%	11.52%	7.69%	6.18%
5		11.52%	8.93%	9.22%	6.93%	5.71%
6		5.76%	8.93%	7.37%	6.23%	5.28%
7			8.93%	6.55%	5.90%	4.89%
8			4.46%	6.55%	5.90%	4.52%
9				6.55%	5.90%	4.46%
10				6.55%	5.90%	4.46%
11				3.29%	5.90%	4.46%
12					5.90%	4.46%
13					5.90%	4.46%
14					5.90%	4.46%
15					5.90%	4.46%
16					3.00%	4.46%
17						4.46%
18						4.46%
19						4.46%
20						4.46%
21						2.25%

NUMBER OF PAYMENTS	2.00%	2.25%	2.50%	2.75%	3.00%	3.25%	3.50%	3.75%	4.00%	4.25%	4.50%	4.75%	5.00%	5.25%	5.50%	5.75%
					(FINANCE CHARGE PER $100 OF AMOUNT FINANCED)											
1	0.17	0.19	0.21	0.23	0.25	0.27	0.29	0.31	0.33	0.35	0.37	0.40	0.42	0.44	0.46	0.48
2	0.25	0.28	0.31	0.34	0.38	0.41	0.44	0.47	0.50	0.53	0.56	0.59	0.63	0.66	0.69	0.72
3	0.33	0.38	0.42	0.46	0.50	0.54	0.58	0.63	0.67	0.71	0.75	0.79	0.83	0.88	0.92	0.96
4	0.42	0.47	0.52	0.57	0.63	0.68	0.73	0.78	0.83	0.89	0.94	0.99	1.04	1.10	1.15	1.20
5	0.50	0.56	0.63	0.69	0.75	0.81	0.88	0.94	1.00	1.07	1.13	1.19	1.25	1.32	1.38	1.44
6	0.58	0.66	0.73	0.80	0.88	0.95	1.02	1.10	1.17	1.24	1.32	1.39	1.46	1.54	1.61	1.68
7	0.67	0.75	0.84	0.92	1.00	1.09	1.17	1.25	1.34	1.42	1.51	1.59	1.67	1.76	1.84	1.93
8	0.75	0.85	0.94	1.03	1.13	1.22	1.32	1.41	1.51	1.60	1.69	1.79	1.88	1.98	2.07	2.17
9	0.84	0.94	1.04	1.15	1.25	1.36	1.46	1.57	1.67	1.78	1.88	1.99	2.09	2.20	2.31	2.41
10	0.92	1.03	1.15	1.26	1.38	1.50	1.61	1.73	1.84	1.96	2.07	2.19	2.31	2.42	2.54	2.65
11	1.00	1.13	1.25	1.38	1.51	1.63	1.76	1.88	2.01	2.14	2.26	2.39	2.52	2.64	2.77	2.90
12	1.09	1.22	1.36	1.50	1.63	1.77	1.91	2.04	2.18	2.32	2.45	2.59	2.73	2.87	3.00	3.14
13	1.17	1.32	1.46	1.61	1.76	1.91	2.05	2.20	2.35	2.50	2.64	2.79	2.94	3.09	3.24	3.39
14	1.25	1.41	1.57	1.73	1.89	2.04	2.20	2.36	2.52	2.68	2.84	2.99	3.15	3.31	3.47	3.63
15	1.34	1.51	1.67	1.84	2.01	2.18	2.35	2.52	2.69	2.86	3.03	3.20	3.37	3.54	3.71	3.88
16	1.42	1.60	1.78	1.96	2.14	2.32	2.50	2.68	2.86	3.04	3.22	3.40	3.58	3.76	3.94	4.12
17	1.51	1.70	1.89	2.08	2.26	2.46	2.65	2.84	3.03	3.22	3.41	3.60	3.79	3.98	4.18	4.37
18	1.59	1.79	1.99	2.19	2.39	2.59	2.79	2.99	3.20	3.40	3.60	3.80	4.00	4.21	4.41	4.61
19	1.67	1.89	2.10	2.31	2.52	2.73	2.94	3.15	3.37	3.58	3.79	4.01	4.22	4.43	4.65	4.86
20	1.76	1.98	2.20	2.42	2.65	2.87	3.09	3.31	3.54	3.76	3.98	4.21	4.43	4.66	4.88	5.11
21	1.84	2.08	2.31	2.54	2.77	3.01	3.24	3.47	3.71	3.94	4.18	4.41	4.65	4.88	5.12	5.35
22	1.93	2.17	2.41	2.66	2.90	3.14	3.39	3.63	3.88	4.12	4.56	4.62	5.11	5.33	5.36	5.60
23	2.01	2.27	2.52	2.77	3.03	3.28	3.54	3.79	4.05	4.31	4.56	4.82	5.08	5.33	5.59	5.85
24	2.10	2.36	2.62	2.89	3.15	3.42	3.69	3.95	4.22	4.49	4.75	5.02	5.29	5.56	5.83	6.10
25	2.18	2.46	2.73	3.01	3.28	3.56	3.84	4.11	4.39	4.67	4.95	5.23	5.51	5.79	6.07	6.35
26	2.27	2.55	2.84	3.12	3.41	3.70	3.99	4.27	4.56	4.85	5.14	5.43	5.72	6.01	6.31	6.60
27	2.35	2.65	2.94	3.24	3.54	3.84	4.13	4.43	4.73	5.03	5.34	5.64	5.94	6.24	6.54	6.85
28	2.43	2.74	3.05	3.36	3.67	3.97	4.28	4.59	4.91	5.22	5.53	5.84	6.15	6.47	6.78	7.10
29	2.52	2.84	3.16	3.47	3.79	4.11	4.43	4.76	5.08	5.40	5.72	6.05	6.37	6.70	7.02	7.35
30	2.60	2.93	3.26	3.59	3.92	4.25	4.58	4.92	5.25	5.58	5.92	6.25	6.59	6.92	7.26	7.60
31	2.69	3.03	3.37	3.71	4.05	4.39	4.73	5.08	5.42	5.77	6.11	6.46	6.81	7.15	7.50	7.85
32	2.77	3.12	3.47	3.83	4.18	4.53	4.88	5.24	5.59	5.95	6.31	6.66	7.02	7.38	7.74	8.10
33	2.86	3.22	3.58	3.94	4.31	4.67	5.04	5.40	5.77	6.13	6.50	6.87	7.24	7.61	7.98	8.35
34	2.94	3.32	3.69	4.06	4.44	4.81	5.19	5.56	5.94	6.32	6.70	7.08	7.46	7.84	8.22	8.61
35	3.03	3.41	3.79	4.18	4.56	4.95	5.34	5.72	6.11	6.50	6.89	7.28	7.68	8.07	8.46	8.86
36	3.11	3.51	3.90	4.30	4.69	5.09	5.49	5.89	6.29	6.69	7.09	7.49	7.90	8.30	8.71	9.11
37	3.20	3.60	4.01	4.41	4.82	5.23	5.64	6.05	6.46	6.87	7.28	7.70	8.11	8.53	8.95	9.37
38	3.28	3.70	4.11	4.53	4.95	5.37	5.79	6.21	6.63	7.06	7.48	7.91	8.33	8.76	9.19	9.62
39	3.37	3.79	4.22	4.65	5.08	5.51	5.94	6.37	6.81	7.24	7.68	8.11	8.55	8.99	9.43	9.87
40	3.45	3.89	4.33	4.77	5.21	5.65	6.09	6.54	6.98	7.43	7.87	8.32	8.77	9.22	9.67	10.13
41	3.54	3.99	4.44	4.89	5.34	5.79	6.24	6.70	7.16	7.61	8.07	8.53	8.99	9.45	9.92	10.38
42	3.62	4.08	4.54	5.00	5.47	5.93	6.40	6.86	7.33	7.80	8.27	8.74	9.21	9.69	10.16	10.64
43	3.71	4.18	4.65	5.12	5.60	6.07	6.55	7.03	7.50	7.98	8.47	8.95	9.43	9.92	10.41	10.89
44	3.79	4.28	4.76	5.24	5.73	6.21	6.70	7.19	7.68	8.17	8.66	9.16	9.65	10.15	10.65	11.15
45	3.88	4.37	4.86	5.36	5.86	6.35	6.85	7.35	7.85	8.36	8.86	9.37	9.88	10.38	10.89	11.41
46	3.97	4.47	4.97	5.48	5.98	6.49	7.00	7.52	8.03	8.54	9.06	9.58	10.10	10.62	11.14	11.66
47	4.05	4.56	5.08	5.60	6.11	6.63	7.16	7.68	8.20	8.73	9.26	9.79	10.32	10.85	11.39	11.92
48	4.14	4.66	5.19	5.72	6.24	6.78	7.31	7.84	8.38	8.92	9.46	10.00	10.54	11.09	11.63	12.18
49	4.22	4.76	5.30	5.83	6.37	6.92	7.46	8.01	8.56	9.10	9.66	10.21	10.76	11.32	11.88	12.44
50	4.31	4.85	5.40	5.95	6.50	7.06	7.61	8.17	8.73	9.29	9.85	10.42	10.99	11.55	12.12	12.70
51	4.39	4.95	5.51	6.07	6.64	7.20	7.77	8.34	8.91	9.48	10.05	10.63	11.21	11.79	12.37	12.95
52	4.48	5.05	5.62	6.19	6.77	7.34	7.92	8.50	9.08	9.67	10.25	10.84	11.43	12.02	12.62	13.21
53	4.56	5.14	5.73	6.31	6.90	7.48	8.07	8.67	9.26	9.86	10.45	11.05	11.66	12.26	12.86	13.47
54	4.65	5.24	5.83	6.43	7.03	7.63	8.23	8.83	9.44	10.04	10.65	11.26	11.88	12.49	13.11	13.73
55	4.74	5.34	5.94	6.55	7.16	7.77	8.38	9.00	9.61	10.23	10.85	11.48	12.10	12.73	13.36	13.99
56	4.82	5.44	6.05	6.67	7.29	7.91	8.53	9.16	9.79	10.42	11.05	11.69	12.33	12.97	13.61	14.25
57	4.91	5.53	6.16	6.79	7.42	8.05	8.69	9.33	9.97	10.61	11.25	11.90	12.55	13.20	13.86	14.52
58	4.99	5.63	6.27	6.91	7.55	8.19	8.84	9.49	10.14	10.80	11.46	12.11	12.78	13.44	14.11	14.78
59	5.08	5.73	6.38	7.03	7.68	8.34	9.00	9.66	10.32	10.99	11.66	12.33	13.00	13.68	14.36	15.04
60	5.17	5.82	6.48	7.15	7.81	8.48	9.15	9.82	10.50	11.18	11.86	12.54	13.23	13.92	14.61	15.30

(FINANCE CHARGE PER $100 OF AMOUNT FINANCED)

NUMBER OF PAYMENTS	6.00%	6.25%	6.50%	6.75%	7.00%	7.25%	7.50%	7.75%	8.00%	8.25%	8.50%	8.75%	9.00%	9.25%	9.50%	9.75%
1	0.50	0.52	0.54	0.56	0.58	0.60	0.62	0.65	0.67	0.69	0.71	0.73	0.75	0.77	0.79	0.81
2	0.75	0.78	0.81	0.84	0.88	0.91	0.94	0.97	1.00	1.03	1.06	1.10	1.13	1.16	1.19	1.22
3	1.00	1.04	1.09	1.13	1.17	1.21	1.25	1.29	1.34	1.38	1.42	1.46	1.50	1.55	1.59	1.63
4	1.25	1.31	1.36	1.41	1.46	1.51	1.57	1.62	1.67	1.72	1.78	1.83	1.88	1.93	1.99	2.04
5	1.50	1.57	1.63	1.69	1.76	1.82	1.88	1.95	2.01	2.07	2.13	2.20	2.26	2.32	2.39	2.45
6	1.76	1.83	1.90	1.98	2.05	2.13	2.20	2.27	2.35	2.42	2.49	2.57	2.64	2.72	2.79	2.86
7	2.01	2.09	2.18	2.26	2.35	2.43	2.52	2.60	2.68	2.77	2.85	2.94	3.02	3.11	3.19	3.28
8	2.26	2.36	2.45	2.55	2.64	2.74	2.83	2.93	3.02	3.12	3.21	3.31	3.40	3.50	3.60	3.69
9	2.52	2.62	2.73	2.83	2.94	3.05	3.15	3.26	3.36	3.47	3.57	3.68	3.79	3.89	4.00	4.11
10	2.77	2.89	3.00	3.12	3.24	3.35	3.47	3.59	3.70	3.82	3.94	4.05	4.17	4.29	4.41	4.52
11	3.02	3.15	3.28	3.41	3.53	3.66	3.79	3.92	4.04	4.17	4.30	4.43	4.56	4.68	4.81	4.94
12	3.28	3.42	3.56	3.69	3.83	3.97	4.11	4.25	4.39	4.52	4.66	4.80	4.94	5.08	5.22	5.36
13	3.53	3.68	3.83	3.98	4.13	4.28	4.43	4.58	4.73	4.88	5.03	5.18	5.33	5.48	5.63	5.78
14	3.79	3.95	4.11	4.27	4.43	4.59	4.75	4.91	5.07	5.23	5.39	5.55	5.72	5.88	6.04	6.20
15	4.05	4.22	4.39	4.56	4.73	4.90	5.07	5.24	5.42	5.59	5.76	5.93	6.10	6.28	6.45	6.62
16	4.30	4.48	4.67	4.85	5.03	5.21	5.40	5.58	5.76	5.94	6.13	6.31	6.49	6.68	6.86	7.05
17	4.56	4.75	4.95	5.14	5.33	5.52	5.72	5.91	6.11	6.30	6.49	6.69	6.88	7.08	7.27	7.47
18	4.82	5.02	5.22	5.43	5.63	5.84	6.04	6.25	6.45	6.66	6.86	7.07	7.28	7.48	7.69	7.90
19	5.07	5.29	5.50	5.72	5.94	6.15	6.37	6.58	6.80	7.02	7.23	7.45	7.67	7.89	8.10	8.32
20	5.33	5.56	5.78	6.01	6.24	6.46	6.69	6.92	7.15	7.38	7.60	7.83	8.06	8.29	8.52	8.75
21	5.59	5.83	6.07	6.30	6.54	6.78	7.02	7.26	7.50	7.74	7.97	8.21	8.46	8.70	8.94	9.18
22	5.85	6.10	6.35	6.60	6.84	7.09	7.34	7.59	7.84	8.10	8.35	8.60	8.85	9.10	9.36	9.61
23	6.11	6.37	6.63	6.89	7.15	7.41	7.67	7.93	8.19	8.46	8.72	8.98	9.25	9.51	9.77	10.04
24	6.37	6.64	6.91	7.18	7.45	7.73	8.00	8.27	8.55	8.82	9.09	9.37	9.64	9.92	10.19	10.47
25	6.63	6.91	7.19	7.48	7.76	8.04	8.33	8.61	8.90	9.18	9.47	9.75	10.04	10.33	10.62	10.90
26	6.89	7.18	7.48	7.77	8.07	8.36	8.66	8.95	9.25	9.55	9.84	10.14	10.44	10.74	11.04	11.34
27	7.15	7.46	7.76	8.07	8.37	8.68	8.99	9.29	9.60	9.91	10.22	10.53	10.84	11.15	11.46	11.77
28	7.41	7.73	8.05	8.36	8.68	9.00	9.32	9.64	9.96	10.28	10.60	10.92	11.24	11.56	11.89	12.21
29	7.67	8.00	8.33	8.66	8.99	9.32	9.65	9.98	10.31	10.64	10.97	11.31	11.64	11.98	12.31	12.65
30	7.94	8.28	8.61	8.96	9.30	9.64	9.98	10.32	10.66	11.01	11.35	11.70	12.04	12.39	12.74	13.09
31	8.20	8.55	8.90	9.25	9.60	9.96	10.31	10.67	11.02	11.38	11.73	12.09	12.45	12.81	13.17	13.53
32	8.46	8.82	9.19	9.55	9.91	10.28	10.64	11.01	11.38	11.74	12.11	12.48	12.85	13.22	13.59	13.97
33	8.73	9.10	9.47	9.85	10.22	10.60	10.98	11.36	11.73	12.11	12.49	12.88	13.26	13.64	14.02	14.41
34	8.99	9.37	9.76	10.15	10.53	10.92	11.31	11.70	12.09	12.48	12.88	13.27	13.66	14.06	14.45	14.85
35	9.25	9.65	10.05	10.45	10.85	11.25	11.65	12.05	12.45	12.85	13.26	13.66	14.07	14.48	14.89	15.29
36	9.52	9.93	10.34	10.75	11.16	11.57	11.98	12.40	12.81	13.23	13.64	14.06	14.48	14.90	15.32	15.74
37	9.78	10.20	10.63	11.05	11.47	11.89	12.32	12.74	13.17	13.60	14.03	14.46	14.89	15.32	15.75	16.19
38	10.05	10.48	10.91	11.35	11.78	12.22	12.66	13.09	13.53	13.97	14.41	14.85	15.30	15.74	16.19	16.63
39	10.32	10.76	11.20	11.65	12.10	12.54	12.99	13.44	13.89	14.35	14.80	15.25	15.71	16.17	16.62	17.08
40	10.58	11.04	11.49	11.95	12.41	12.87	13.33	13.79	14.26	14.72	15.19	15.65	16.12	16.59	17.06	17.53
41	10.85	11.32	11.78	12.25	12.72	13.20	13.67	14.14	14.62	15.10	15.57	16.05	16.53	17.01	17.50	17.98
42	11.12	11.60	12.08	12.56	13.04	13.52	14.01	14.50	14.98	15.47	15.96	16.45	16.95	17.44	17.94	18.43
43	11.38	11.87	12.37	12.86	13.36	13.85	14.35	14.85	15.35	15.85	16.35	16.86	17.36	17.87	18.38	18.89
44	11.65	12.15	12.66	13.16	13.67	14.18	14.69	15.20	15.71	16.23	16.74	17.26	17.78	18.30	18.82	19.34
45	11.92	12.44	12.95	13.47	13.99	14.51	15.03	15.55	16.08	16.61	17.13	17.66	18.19	18.73	19.26	19.79
46	12.19	12.72	13.24	13.77	14.31	14.84	15.37	15.91	16.45	16.99	17.53	18.07	18.61	19.16	19.70	20.25
47	12.46	13.00	13.54	14.08	14.62	15.17	15.72	16.26	16.81	17.37	17.92	18.47	19.03	19.59	20.15	20.71
48	12.73	13.28	13.83	14.39	14.94	15.50	16.06	16.62	17.18	17.75	18.31	18.88	19.45	20.02	20.59	21.16
49	13.00	13.56	14.13	14.69	15.26	15.83	16.40	16.98	17.55	18.13	18.71	19.29	19.87	20.45	21.04	21.62
50	13.27	13.84	14.42	15.00	15.58	16.16	16.75	17.33	17.92	18.51	19.10	19.69	20.29	20.89	21.48	22.08
51	13.54	14.13	14.72	15.31	15.90	16.50	17.09	17.69	18.29	18.89	19.50	20.10	20.71	21.32	21.93	22.55
52	13.81	14.41	15.01	15.62	16.22	16.83	17.44	18.05	18.66	19.28	19.89	20.51	21.13	21.76	22.38	23.01
53	14.08	14.69	15.31	15.92	16.54	17.16	17.78	18.41	19.03	19.66	20.29	20.92	21.56	22.19	22.83	23.47
54	14.36	14.98	15.61	16.23	16.86	17.50	18.13	18.77	19.41	20.05	20.69	21.34	21.98	22.63	23.28	23.94
55	14.63	15.26	15.90	16.54	17.19	17.83	18.48	19.13	19.78	20.43	21.09	21.75	22.41	23.07	23.73	24.40
56	14.90	15.55	16.20	16.85	17.51	18.17	18.83	19.49	20.15	20.82	21.49	22.16	22.83	23.51	24.19	24.87
57	15.17	15.84	16.50	17.17	17.83	18.50	19.18	19.85	20.53	21.21	21.89	22.58	23.26	23.95	24.64	25.34
58	15.45	16.12	16.80	17.48	18.16	18.84	19.53	20.21	20.91	21.60	22.29	22.99	23.69	24.39	25.10	25.80
59	15.72	16.41	17.10	17.79	18.48	19.18	19.88	20.58	21.28	21.99	22.70	23.41	24.12	24.84	25.55	26.27
60	16.00	16.70	17.40	18.10	18.81	19.52	20.23	20.94	21.66	22.38	23.10	23.82	24.55	25.28	26.01	26.75

NUMBER OF PAYMENTS	ANNUAL PERCENTAGE RATE															
	10.00%	10.25%	10.50%	10.75%	11.00%	11.25%	11.50%	11.75%	12.00%	12.25%	12.50%	12.75%	13.00%	13.25%	13.50%	13.75%

(FINANCE CHARGE PER $100 OF AMOUNT FINANCED)

NUMBER OF PAYMENTS	10.00%	10.25%	10.50%	10.75%	11.00%	11.25%	11.50%	11.75%	12.00%	12.25%	12.50%	12.75%	13.00%	13.25%	13.50%	13.75%
1	0.83	0.85	0.87	0.90	0.92	0.94	0.96	0.98	1.00	1.02	1.04	1.06	1.08	1.10	1.12	1.15
2	1.25	1.28	1.31	1.35	1.38	1.41	1.44	1.47	1.50	1.53	1.57	1.60	1.63	1.66	1.69	1.72
3	1.67	1.71	1.76	1.80	1.84	1.88	1.92	1.96	2.01	2.05	2.09	2.13	2.17	2.22	2.26	2.30
4	2.09	2.14	2.20	2.25	2.30	2.35	2.41	2.46	2.51	2.57	2.62	2.67	2.72	2.78	2.83	2.88
5	2.51	2.58	2.64	2.70	2.77	2.83	2.89	2.96	3.02	3.08	3.15	3.21	3.27	3.34	3.40	3.46
6	2.94	3.01	3.08	3.16	3.23	3.31	3.38	3.45	3.53	3.60	3.68	3.75	3.83	3.90	3.97	4.05
7	3.36	3.45	3.53	3.62	3.70	3.78	3.87	3.95	4.04	4.12	4.21	4.29	4.38	4.47	4.55	4.64
8	3.79	3.88	3.98	4.07	4.17	4.26	4.36	4.46	4.55	4.65	4.74	4.84	4.94	5.03	5.13	5.22
9	4.21	4.32	4.43	4.53	4.64	4.75	4.85	4.96	5.07	5.17	5.28	5.39	5.49	5.60	5.71	5.82
10	4.64	4.76	4.88	4.99	5.11	5.23	5.35	5.46	5.58	5.70	5.82	5.94	6.05	6.17	6.29	6.41
11	5.07	5.20	5.33	5.45	5.58	5.71	5.84	5.97	6.10	6.23	6.36	6.49	6.62	6.75	6.88	7.01
12	5.50	5.64	5.78	5.92	6.06	6.20	6.34	6.48	6.62	6.76	6.90	7.04	7.18	7.32	7.46	7.60
13	5.93	6.08	6.23	6.38	6.53	6.68	6.84	6.99	7.14	7.29	7.44	7.59	7.75	7.90	8.05	8.20
14	6.36	6.52	6.69	6.85	7.01	7.17	7.34	7.50	7.66	7.82	7.99	8.15	8.31	8.48	8.64	8.81
15	6.80	6.97	7.14	7.32	7.49	7.66	7.84	8.01	8.19	8.36	8.53	8.71	8.88	9.06	9.23	9.41
16	7.23	7.41	7.60	7.78	7.97	8.15	8.34	8.53	8.71	8.90	9.08	9.27	9.46	9.64	9.83	10.02
17	7.67	7.86	8.06	8.25	8.45	8.65	8.84	9.04	9.24	9.44	9.63	9.83	10.03	10.23	10.43	10.63
18	8.10	8.31	8.52	8.73	8.93	9.14	9.35	9.56	9.77	9.98	10.19	10.40	10.61	10.82	11.03	11.24
19	8.54	8.76	8.98	9.20	9.42	9.64	9.86	10.08	10.30	10.52	10.74	10.96	11.18	11.41	11.63	11.85
20	8.98	9.21	9.44	9.67	9.90	10.13	10.37	10.60	10.83	11.06	11.30	11.53	11.76	12.00	12.23	12.46
21	9.42	9.66	9.90	10.15	10.39	10.63	10.88	11.12	11.36	11.61	11.85	12.10	12.34	12.59	12.84	13.08
22	9.86	10.12	10.37	10.62	10.88	11.13	11.39	11.64	11.90	12.16	12.41	12.67	12.93	13.19	13.44	13.70
23	10.30	10.57	10.84	11.10	11.37	11.63	11.90	12.17	12.44	12.71	12.97	13.24	13.51	13.78	14.05	14.32
24	10.75	11.02	11.30	11.58	11.86	12.14	12.42	12.70	12.98	13.26	13.54	13.82	14.10	14.38	14.66	14.95
25	11.19	11.48	11.77	12.06	12.35	12.64	12.93	13.22	13.52	13.81	14.10	14.40	14.69	14.98	15.28	15.57
26	11.64	11.94	12.24	12.54	12.85	13.15	13.45	13.75	14.06	14.36	14.67	14.97	15.28	15.59	15.89	16.20
27	12.09	12.40	12.71	13.03	13.34	13.66	13.97	14.29	14.60	14.92	15.24	15.56	15.87	16.19	16.51	16.83
28	12.53	12.86	13.18	13.51	13.84	14.16	14.49	14.82	15.15	15.48	15.81	16.14	16.47	16.80	17.13	17.46
29	12.98	13.32	13.66	14.00	14.33	14.67	15.01	15.35	15.70	16.04	16.38	16.72	17.07	17.41	17.75	18.10
30	13.43	13.78	14.13	14.48	14.83	15.19	15.54	15.89	16.24	16.60	16.95	17.31	17.66	18.02	18.38	18.74
31	13.89	14.25	14.61	14.97	15.33	15.70	16.06	16.43	16.79	17.16	17.53	17.90	18.27	18.63	19.00	19.38
32	14.34	14.71	15.09	15.46	15.84	16.21	16.59	16.97	17.35	17.73	18.11	18.49	18.87	19.25	19.63	20.02
33	14.79	15.18	15.57	15.95	16.34	16.73	17.12	17.51	17.90	18.29	18.69	19.08	19.47	19.87	20.26	20.66
34	15.25	15.65	16.05	16.44	16.85	17.25	17.65	18.05	18.46	18.86	19.27	19.67	20.08	20.49	20.90	21.31
35	15.70	16.11	16.53	16.94	17.35	17.77	18.18	18.60	19.01	19.43	19.85	20.27	20.69	21.11	21.53	21.95
36	16.16	16.58	17.01	17.43	17.86	18.29	18.71	19.14	19.57	20.00	20.43	20.87	21.30	21.73	22.17	22.60
37	16.62	17.06	17.49	17.93	18.37	18.81	19.25	19.69	20.13	20.58	21.02	21.46	21.91	22.36	22.81	23.25
38	17.08	17.53	17.98	18.43	18.88	19.33	19.78	20.24	20.69	21.15	21.61	22.07	22.52	22.99	23.45	23.91
39	17.54	18.00	18.46	18.93	19.39	19.86	20.32	20.79	21.26	21.73	22.20	22.67	23.14	23.61	24.09	24.56
40	18.00	18.48	18.95	19.43	19.90	20.38	20.86	21.34	21.82	22.30	22.79	23.27	23.76	24.25	24.73	25.22
41	18.47	18.95	19.44	19.93	20.42	20.91	21.40	21.89	22.39	22.88	23.38	23.88	24.38	24.88	25.38	25.88
42	18.93	19.43	19.93	20.43	20.93	21.44	21.94	22.45	22.96	23.47	23.98	24.49	25.00	25.51	26.03	26.55
43	19.40	19.91	20.42	20.94	21.45	21.97	22.49	23.01	23.53	24.05	24.57	25.10	25.62	26.15	26.68	27.21
44	19.86	20.39	20.91	21.44	21.97	22.50	23.03	23.57	24.10	24.64	25.17	25.71	26.25	26.79	27.33	27.88
45	20.33	20.87	21.41	21.95	22.49	23.03	23.58	24.12	24.67	25.22	25.77	26.32	26.88	27.43	27.99	28.55
46	20.80	21.35	21.90	22.46	23.01	23.57	24.13	24.69	25.25	25.81	26.37	26.94	27.51	28.08	28.65	29.22
47	21.27	21.83	22.40	22.97	23.53	24.10	24.68	25.25	25.82	26.40	26.98	27.56	28.14	28.72	29.31	29.89
48	21.74	22.32	22.90	23.48	24.06	24.64	25.23	25.81	26.40	26.99	27.58	28.18	28.77	29.37	29.97	30.57
49	22.21	22.80	23.39	23.99	24.58	25.18	25.78	26.38	26.98	27.59	28.19	28.80	29.41	30.02	30.63	31.24
50	22.69	23.29	23.89	24.50	25.11	25.72	26.33	26.95	27.56	28.18	28.80	29.42	30.04	30.67	31.29	31.92
51	23.16	23.78	24.40	25.02	25.64	26.26	26.89	27.52	28.15	28.78	29.41	30.05	30.68	31.32	31.96	32.60
52	23.64	24.27	24.90	25.53	26.17	26.81	27.45	28.09	28.73	29.38	30.02	30.67	31.32	31.98	32.63	33.29
53	24.11	24.76	25.40	26.05	26.70	27.35	28.00	28.66	29.32	29.98	30.64	31.30	31.97	32.63	33.30	33.97
54	24.59	25.25	25.91	26.57	27.23	27.90	28.56	29.23	29.91	30.58	31.25	31.93	32.61	33.29	33.98	34.66
55	25.07	25.74	26.41	27.09	27.77	28.44	29.13	29.81	30.50	31.18	31.87	32.56	33.26	33.95	34.65	35.35
56	25.55	26.23	26.92	27.61	28.30	28.99	29.69	30.39	31.09	31.79	32.49	33.20	33.91	34.62	35.33	36.04
57	26.03	26.73	27.43	28.13	28.84	29.54	30.25	30.97	31.68	32.39	33.11	33.83	34.56	35.28	36.01	36.74
58	26.51	27.23	27.94	28.66	29.37	30.10	30.82	31.55	32.27	33.00	33.74	34.47	35.21	35.95	36.69	37.43
59	27.00	27.72	28.45	29.18	29.91	30.65	31.39	32.13	32.87	33.61	34.36	35.11	35.86	36.62	37.37	38.13
60	27.48	28.22	28.96	29.71	30.45	31.20	31.96	32.71	33.47	34.23	34.99	35.75	36.52	37.29	38.06	38.83

NUMBER OF PAYMENTS	14.00%	14.25%	14.50%	14.75%	15.00%	15.25%	15.50%	15.75%	16.00%	16.25%	16.50%	16.75%	17.00%	17.25%	17.50%	17.75%
	(FINANCE CHARGE PER $100 OF AMOUNT FINANCED)															
1	1.17	1.19	1.21	1.23	1.25	1.27	1.29	1.31	1.33	1.35	1.37	1.40	1.42	1.44	1.46	1.48
2	1.75	1.78	1.82	1.85	1.88	1.91	1.94	1.97	2.00	2.04	2.07	2.10	2.13	2.16	2.19	2.22
3	2.34	2.38	2.43	2.47	2.51	2.55	2.59	2.64	2.68	2.72	2.76	2.80	2.85	2.89	2.93	2.97
4	2.93	2.99	3.04	3.09	3.14	3.20	3.25	3.30	3.36	3.41	3.46	3.51	3.57	3.62	3.67	3.73
5	3.53	3.59	3.65	3.72	3.78	3.84	3.91	3.97	4.04	4.10	4.16	4.23	4.29	4.35	4.42	4.48
6	4.12	4.20	4.27	4.35	4.42	4.49	4.57	4.64	4.72	4.79	4.87	4.94	5.02	5.09	5.17	5.24
7	4.72	4.81	4.89	4.98	5.06	5.15	5.23	5.32	5.40	5.49	5.58	5.66	5.75	5.83	5.92	6.00
8	5.32	5.42	5.51	5.61	5.71	5.80	5.90	6.00	6.09	6.19	6.29	6.38	6.48	6.58	6.67	6.77
9	5.92	6.03	6.14	6.25	6.35	6.46	6.57	6.68	6.78	6.89	7.00	7.11	7.22	7.32	7.43	7.54
10	6.53	6.65	6.77	6.88	7.00	7.12	7.24	7.36	7.48	7.60	7.72	7.84	7.96	8.08	8.19	8.31
11	7.14	7.27	7.40	7.53	7.66	7.79	7.92	8.05	8.18	8.31	8.44	8.57	8.70	8.83	8.96	9.09
12	7.74	7.89	8.03	8.17	8.31	8.45	8.59	8.74	8.88	9.02	9.16	9.30	9.45	9.59	9.73	9.87
13	8.36	8.51	8.66	8.81	8.97	9.12	9.27	9.43	9.58	9.73	9.89	10.04	10.20	10.35	10.50	10.66
14	8.97	9.13	9.30	9.46	9.63	9.79	9.96	10.12	10.29	10.45	10.62	10.78	10.95	11.11	11.28	11.45
15	9.59	9.76	9.94	10.11	10.29	10.47	10.64	10.82	11.00	11.17	11.35	11.53	11.71	11.88	12.06	12.24
16	10.20	10.39	10.58	10.77	10.95	11.14	11.33	11.52	11.71	11.90	12.09	12.28	12.46	12.65	12.84	13.03
17	10.82	11.02	11.22	11.42	11.62	11.82	12.02	12.22	12.42	12.62	12.83	13.03	13.23	13.43	13.63	13.83
18	11.45	11.66	11.87	12.08	12.29	12.50	12.72	12.93	13.14	13.35	13.57	13.78	13.99	14.21	14.42	14.64
19	12.07	12.30	12.52	12.74	12.97	13.19	13.41	13.64	13.86	14.09	14.31	14.54	14.76	14.99	15.22	15.44
20	12.70	12.93	13.17	13.41	13.64	13.88	14.11	14.35	14.59	14.82	15.06	15.30	15.54	15.77	16.01	16.25
21	13.33	13.58	13.82	14.07	14.32	14.57	14.82	15.06	15.31	15.56	15.81	16.06	16.31	16.56	16.81	17.07
22	13.96	14.22	14.48	14.74	15.00	15.26	15.52	15.78	16.04	16.30	16.57	16.83	17.09	17.36	17.62	17.88
23	14.59	14.87	15.14	15.41	15.68	15.96	16.23	16.50	16.78	17.05	17.32	17.60	17.88	18.15	18.43	18.70
24	15.23	15.51	15.80	16.08	16.37	16.65	16.94	17.22	17.51	17.80	18.09	18.37	18.66	18.95	19.24	19.53
25	15.87	16.17	16.46	16.76	17.06	17.35	17.65	17.95	18.25	18.55	18.85	19.15	19.45	19.75	20.05	20.36
26	16.51	16.82	17.13	17.44	17.75	18.06	18.37	18.68	18.99	19.30	19.62	19.93	20.24	20.56	20.87	21.19
27	17.15	17.47	17.80	18.12	18.44	18.76	19.09	19.41	19.74	20.06	20.39	20.71	21.04	21.37	21.69	22.02
28	17.80	18.13	18.47	18.80	19.14	19.47	19.81	20.15	20.48	20.82	21.16	21.50	21.84	22.18	22.52	22.86
29	18.45	18.79	19.14	19.49	19.83	20.18	20.53	20.89	21.23	21.58	21.94	22.29	22.64	22.99	23.35	23.70
30	19.10	19.45	19.81	20.17	20.54	20.90	21.26	21.62	21.99	22.35	22.72	23.08	23.45	23.81	24.18	24.55
31	19.75	20.12	20.49	20.87	21.24	21.61	21.99	22.37	22.74	23.12	23.50	23.88	24.26	24.64	25.02	25.40
32	20.40	20.79	21.17	21.56	21.95	22.33	22.72	23.11	23.50	23.89	24.28	24.68	25.07	25.46	25.86	26.25
33	21.06	21.46	21.85	22.25	22.65	23.06	23.46	23.86	24.26	24.67	25.07	25.48	25.88	26.29	26.70	27.11
34	21.72	22.13	22.54	22.95	23.37	23.78	24.19	24.61	25.03	25.44	25.86	26.28	26.70	27.12	27.54	27.97
35	22.38	22.80	23.23	23.65	24.08	24.51	24.94	25.36	25.79	26.23	26.66	27.09	27.52	27.96	28.39	28.83
36	23.04	23.48	23.92	24.35	24.80	25.24	25.68	26.12	26.57	27.01	27.46	27.90	28.35	28.80	29.25	29.70
37	23.70	24.16	24.61	25.06	25.51	25.97	26.42	26.88	27.34	27.80	28.26	28.72	29.18	29.64	30.10	30.57
38	24.37	24.84	25.30	25.77	26.24	26.70	27.17	27.64	28.11	28.59	29.06	29.53	30.01	30.49	30.96	31.44
39	25.04	25.52	26.00	26.48	26.96	27.44	27.92	28.41	28.89	29.38	29.87	30.36	30.85	31.34	31.83	32.32
40	25.71	26.20	26.70	27.19	27.69	28.18	28.68	29.18	29.68	30.18	30.68	31.19	31.68	32.19	32.69	33.20
41	26.39	26.89	27.40	27.91	28.41	28.92	29.44	29.95	30.46	30.97	31.49	32.01	32.52	33.04	33.56	34.08
42	27.06	27.58	28.10	28.62	29.15	29.67	30.19	30.72	31.25	31.78	32.31	32.84	33.37	33.90	34.44	34.97
43	27.74	28.27	28.81	29.34	29.88	30.42	30.96	31.50	32.04	32.58	33.13	33.67	34.22	34.76	35.31	35.86
44	28.42	28.97	29.52	30.07	30.62	31.17	31.72	32.28	32.83	33.39	33.95	34.51	35.07	35.63	36.19	36.76
45	29.11	29.67	30.23	30.79	31.36	31.92	32.49	33.06	33.63	34.20	34.77	35.35	35.92	36.50	37.08	37.66
46	29.79	30.36	30.94	31.52	32.10	32.68	33.26	33.84	34.43	35.01	35.60	36.19	36.78	37.37	37.96	38.56
47	30.48	31.07	31.66	32.25	32.84	33.44	34.03	34.63	35.23	35.83	36.43	37.04	37.64	38.25	38.86	39.46
48	31.17	31.77	32.37	32.98	33.59	34.20	34.81	35.42	36.03	36.65	37.27	37.88	38.50	39.13	39.75	40.37
49	31.86	32.48	33.09	33.71	34.34	34.96	35.59	36.21	36.84	37.47	38.10	38.74	39.37	40.01	40.65	41.29
50	32.55	33.18	33.82	34.45	35.09	35.73	36.37	37.01	37.65	38.30	38.94	39.59	40.24	40.89	41.55	42.20
51	33.25	33.89	34.54	35.19	35.84	36.49	37.15	37.81	38.46	39.12	39.79	40.45	41.11	41.78	42.45	43.12
52	33.95	34.61	35.27	35.93	36.60	37.27	37.94	38.61	39.28	39.96	40.63	41.31	41.99	42.67	43.36	44.04
53	34.65	35.32	36.00	36.68	37.36	38.04	38.72	39.41	40.10	40.79	41.48	42.17	42.87	43.57	44.27	44.97
54	35.35	36.04	36.73	37.42	38.12	38.82	39.52	40.22	40.92	41.63	42.33	43.04	43.75	44.47	45.18	45.90
55	36.05	36.76	37.46	38.17	38.88	39.60	40.31	41.03	41.74	42.47	43.19	43.91	44.64	45.37	46.10	46.83
56	36.76	37.48	38.20	38.92	39.65	40.38	41.11	41.84	42.57	43.31	44.05	44.79	45.53	46.27	47.02	47.77
57	37.47	38.20	38.94	39.68	40.42	41.16	41.91	42.65	43.40	44.15	44.91	45.66	46.42	47.18	47.94	48.71
58	38.18	38.93	39.68	40.43	41.19	41.95	42.71	43.47	44.23	45.00	45.77	46.54	47.32	48.09	48.87	49.65
59	38.89	39.66	40.42	41.19	41.96	42.74	43.51	44.29	45.07	45.85	46.64	47.42	48.21	49.01	49.80	50.60
60	39.61	40.39	41.17	41.95	42.74	43.53	44.32	45.11	45.91	46.71	47.51	48.31	49.12	49.92	50.73	51.55

NUMBER OF PAYMENTS	ANNUAL PERCENTAGE RATE															
	18.00%	18.25%	18.50%	18.75%	19.00%	19.25%	19.50%	19.75%	20.00%	20.25%	20.50%	20.75%	21.00%	21.25%	21.50%	21.75%
	(FINANCE CHARGE PER $100 OF AMOUNT FINANCED)															
1	1.50	1.52	1.54	1.56	1.58	1.60	1.62	1.65	1.67	1.69	1.71	1.73	1.75	1.77	1.79	1.81
2	2.26	2.29	2.32	2.35	2.38	2.41	2.44	2.48	2.51	2.54	2.57	2.60	2.63	2.66	2.70	2.73
3	3.01	3.06	3.10	3.14	3.18	3.23	3.27	3.31	3.35	3.39	3.44	3.48	3.52	3.56	3.60	3.65
4	3.78	3.83	3.88	3.94	3.99	4.04	4.10	4.15	4.20	4.25	4.31	4.36	4.41	4.47	4.52	4.57
5	4.54	4.61	4.67	4.74	4.80	4.86	4.93	4.99	5.06	5.12	5.18	5.25	5.31	5.37	5.44	5.50
6	5.32	5.39	5.46	5.54	5.61	5.69	5.76	5.84	5.91	5.99	6.06	6.14	6.21	6.29	6.36	6.44
7	6.09	6.18	6.26	6.35	6.43	6.52	6.60	6.69	6.78	6.86	6.95	7.04	7.12	7.21	7.29	7.38
8	6.87	6.96	7.06	7.16	7.26	7.35	7.45	7.55	7.64	7.74	7.84	7.94	8.03	8.13	8.23	8.33
9	7.65	7.76	7.87	7.97	8.08	8.19	8.30	8.41	8.52	8.63	8.73	8.84	8.95	9.06	9.17	9.28
10	8.43	8.55	8.67	8.79	8.91	9.03	9.15	9.27	9.39	9.51	9.63	9.75	9.88	10.00	10.12	10.24
11	9.22	9.35	9.49	9.62	9.75	9.88	10.01	10.14	10.28	10.41	10.54	10.67	10.80	10.94	11.07	11.20
12	10.02	10.16	10.30	10.44	10.59	10.73	10.87	11.02	11.16	11.31	11.45	11.59	11.74	11.88	12.02	12.17
13	10.81	10.97	11.12	11.28	11.43	11.59	11.74	11.90	12.05	12.21	12.36	12.52	12.67	12.83	12.99	13.14
14	11.61	11.78	11.95	12.11	12.28	12.45	12.61	12.78	12.95	13.11	13.28	13.45	13.62	13.79	13.95	14.12
15	12.42	12.59	12.77	12.95	13.13	13.31	13.49	13.67	13.85	14.03	14.21	14.39	14.57	14.75	14.93	15.11
16	13.22	13.41	13.60	13.80	13.99	14.18	14.37	14.56	14.75	14.94	15.13	15.33	15.52	15.71	15.90	16.10
17	14.04	14.24	14.44	14.64	14.85	15.05	15.25	15.46	15.66	15.86	16.07	16.27	16.48	16.68	16.89	17.09
18	14.85	15.07	15.28	15.49	15.71	15.93	16.14	16.36	16.57	16.79	17.01	17.22	17.44	17.66	17.88	18.09
19	15.67	15.90	16.12	16.35	16.58	16.81	17.03	17.26	17.49	17.72	17.95	18.18	18.41	18.64	18.87	19.10
20	16.49	16.73	16.97	17.21	17.45	17.69	17.93	18.17	18.41	18.66	18.90	19.14	19.38	19.63	19.87	20.11
21	17.32	17.57	17.82	18.07	18.33	18.58	18.83	19.09	19.34	19.60	19.85	20.11	20.36	20.62	20.87	21.13
22	18.15	18.41	18.68	18.94	19.21	19.47	19.74	20.01	20.27	20.54	20.81	21.08	21.34	21.61	21.88	22.15
23	18.98	19.26	19.54	19.81	20.09	20.37	20.65	20.93	21.21	21.49	21.77	22.05	22.33	22.61	22.90	23.18
24	19.82	20.11	20.40	20.69	20.98	21.27	21.56	21.86	22.15	22.44	22.74	23.03	23.33	23.62	23.92	24.21
25	20.66	20.96	21.27	21.57	21.87	22.18	22.48	22.79	23.10	23.40	23.71	24.02	24.32	24.63	24.94	25.25
26	21.50	21.82	22.14	22.45	22.77	23.09	23.41	23.73	24.04	24.36	24.68	25.01	25.33	25.65	25.97	26.29
27	22.35	22.68	23.01	23.34	23.67	24.00	24.33	24.67	25.00	25.33	25.67	26.00	26.34	26.67	27.01	27.34
28	23.20	23.55	23.89	24.23	24.58	24.92	25.27	25.61	25.96	26.30	26.65	27.00	27.35	27.70	28.05	28.40
29	24.06	24.41	24.77	25.13	25.49	25.84	26.20	26.56	26.92	27.28	27.64	28.00	28.37	28.73	29.09	29.46
30	24.92	25.29	25.66	26.03	26.40	26.77	27.14	27.52	27.89	28.26	28.64	29.01	29.39	29.77	30.14	30.52
31	25.78	26.16	26.55	26.93	27.32	27.70	28.09	28.47	28.86	29.25	29.64	30.03	30.42	30.81	31.20	31.59
32	26.65	27.04	27.44	27.84	28.24	28.64	29.04	29.44	29.84	30.24	30.64	31.05	31.45	31.85	32.26	32.67
33	27.52	27.93	28.34	28.75	29.16	29.57	29.99	30.40	30.82	31.23	31.65	32.07	32.49	32.91	33.33	33.75
34	28.39	28.81	29.24	29.66	30.09	30.52	30.95	31.37	31.80	32.23	32.67	33.10	33.53	33.96	34.40	34.83
35	29.27	29.71	30.14	30.58	31.02	31.47	31.91	32.35	32.79	33.24	33.68	34.13	34.58	35.03	35.47	35.92
36	30.15	30.60	31.05	31.51	31.96	32.42	32.87	33.33	33.79	34.25	34.71	35.17	35.63	36.09	36.56	37.02
37	31.03	31.50	31.97	32.43	32.90	33.37	33.84	34.32	34.79	35.26	35.74	36.21	36.69	37.16	37.64	38.12
38	31.92	32.40	32.88	33.37	33.85	34.33	34.82	35.30	35.79	36.28	36.77	37.26	37.75	38.24	38.73	39.23
39	32.81	33.31	33.80	34.30	34.80	35.30	35.80	36.30	36.80	37.30	37.81	38.31	38.82	39.32	39.83	40.34
40	33.71	34.22	34.73	35.24	35.75	36.26	36.78	37.29	37.81	38.33	38.85	39.37	39.89	40.41	40.93	41.46
41	34.61	35.13	35.66	36.18	36.71	37.24	37.77	38.30	38.83	39.36	39.89	40.43	40.96	41.50	42.04	42.58
42	35.51	36.05	36.59	37.13	37.67	38.21	38.76	39.30	39.85	40.40	40.95	41.50	42.05	42.60	43.15	43.71
43	36.42	36.97	37.52	38.08	38.63	39.19	39.75	40.31	40.87	41.44	42.00	42.57	43.13	43.70	44.27	44.84
44	37.33	37.89	38.46	39.03	39.60	40.18	40.75	41.33	41.90	42.48	43.06	43.64	44.22	44.81	45.39	45.98
45	38.24	38.82	39.41	39.99	40.58	41.17	41.75	42.35	42.94	43.53	44.13	44.72	45.32	45.92	46.52	47.12
46	39.16	39.75	40.35	40.95	41.55	42.16	42.76	43.37	43.98	44.58	45.20	45.81	46.42	47.03	47.65	48.27
47	40.08	40.69	41.30	41.92	42.54	43.15	43.77	44.40	45.02	45.64	46.27	46.90	47.53	48.16	48.79	49.42
48	41.00	41.63	42.26	42.89	43.52	44.15	44.79	45.43	46.07	46.71	47.35	47.99	48.64	49.28	49.93	50.58
49	41.93	42.57	43.22	43.86	44.51	45.16	45.81	46.46	47.12	47.77	48.43	49.09	49.75	50.41	51.08	51.74
50	42.86	43.52	44.18	44.84	45.50	46.17	46.83	47.50	48.17	48.84	49.52	50.19	50.87	51.55	52.23	52.91
51	43.79	44.47	45.14	45.82	46.50	47.18	47.86	48.55	49.23	49.92	50.61	51.30	51.99	52.69	53.38	54.08
52	44.73	45.42	46.11	46.80	47.50	48.20	48.89	49.59	50.30	51.00	51.71	52.41	53.12	53.83	54.55	55.26
53	45.67	46.38	47.08	47.79	48.50	49.22	49.93	50.65	51.37	52.09	52.81	53.53	54.26	54.98	55.71	56.44
54	46.62	47.34	48.06	48.79	49.51	50.24	50.97	51.70	52.44	53.17	53.91	54.65	55.39	56.14	56.88	57.63
55	47.57	48.30	49.04	49.78	50.52	51.27	52.02	52.76	53.52	54.27	55.02	55.78	56.54	57.30	58.06	58.82
56	48.52	49.27	50.03	50.78	51.54	52.30	53.06	53.83	54.60	55.37	56.14	56.91	57.68	58.46	59.24	60.02
57	49.47	50.24	51.01	51.79	52.56	53.34	54.12	54.90	55.68	56.47	57.25	58.04	58.84	59.63	60.43	61.22
58	50.43	51.22	52.00	52.79	53.58	54.38	55.17	55.97	56.77	57.57	58.38	59.18	59.99	60.80	61.62	62.43
59	51.39	52.20	53.00	53.80	54.61	55.42	56.23	57.05	57.87	58.68	59.51	60.33	61.15	61.98	62.81	63.64
60	52.36	53.18	54.00	54.82	55.64	56.47	57.30	58.13	58.96	59.80	60.64	61.48	62.32	63.17	64.01	64.86

LIFE INSURANCE RATES*

Age	Five-year term	Age	Straight life	Age	Twenty-payment life	Age	Twenty-year endowment
20	1.85	20	5.90	20	8.28	20	13.85
21	1.85	21	6.13	21	8.61	21	14.35
22	1.85	22	6.35	22	8.91	22	14.92
23	1.85	23	6.60	23	9.23	23	15.54
24	1.85	24	6.85	24	9.56	24	16.05
25	1.85	25	7.13	25	9.91	25	17.55
26	1.85	26	7.43	26	10.29	26	17.66
27	1.86	27	7.75	27	10.70	27	18.33
28	1.86	28	8.08	28	11.12	28	19.12
29	1.87	29	8.46	29	11.58	29	20.00
30	1.87	30	8.85	30	12.05	30	20.90
31	1.87	31	9.27	31	12.57	31	21.88
32	1.88	32	9.71	32	13.10	32	22.89
33	1.95	33	10.20	33	13.67	33	23.98
34	2.08	34	10.71	34	14.28	34	25.13
35	2.23	35	11.26	35	14.92	35	26.35
36	2.44	36	11.84	36	15.60	36	27.64
37	2.67	37	12.46	37	16.30	37	28.97
38	2.95	38	13.12	38	17.04	38	30.38
39	3.24	39	13.81	39	17.81	39	31.84
40	3.52	40	14.54	40	18.61	40	33.36
41	3.79	41	15.30	41	19.44	41	34.94
42	4.04	42	16.11	42	20.31	42	36.59
43	4.26	43	16.96	43	21.21	43	38.29
44	4.50	44	17.86	44	22.15	44	40.09

*Note these tables are a sampling of age groups, premium costs, and insurance coverage that are available over 44 years of age.

NONFORFEITURE OPTIONS BASED ON $1,000 FACE VALUE

Years insurance policy in force	Straight life		Extended term		Twenty-payment life		Extended term		Twenty-year endowment		Extended term	
	Cash value	Amount of paid-up insurance	Years	Day	Cash value	Amount of paid-up insurance	Years	Day	Cash value	Amount of paid-up insurance	Years	Day
5	29	86	9	91	71	220	19	190	92	229	23	140
10	96	259	18	76	186	521	28	195	319	520	30	160
15	148	371	20	165	317	781	32	176	610	790	35	300
20	265	550	21	300	475	1,000	Life		1,000	1,000	Life	

COMPULSORY INSURANCE (BASED ON CLASS OF DRIVER)

Bodily injury to others		Damage to someone else's property	
Class	10/20	Class	5M
10	$ 55	10	129
17	98	17	160
18	80	18	160
20	116	20	186

DAMAGE TO SOMEONE ELSE'S PROPERTY

Class	10M	25M	50M	100M
10	132	134	135	136
17	164	166	168	169
18	164	166	168	169
20	191	193	195	197

TOWING AND SUBSTITUTE TRANSPORATION

Towing and labor	$ 4
Substitute transportation	16

FIRE INSURANCE RATES PER $100 OF COVERAGE FOR BUILDINGS AND CONTENTS

Rating of area	Classification of building			
	Class A		Class B	
	Buildings	Contents	Buildings	Contents
1	.28	.35	.41	.54
2	.33	.47	.50	.60
3	.41	.50	.61	.65

FIRE INSURANCE SHORT-RATE AND CANCELLATION TABLE

Time policy in force	Percent of annual rate to be charged	Time policy in force	Percent of annual rate to be charged	Time policy in force	Percent of annual rate to be charged
Days: 5	8%	Months: 3	35	Months: 8	74
10	10	4	44	9	81
20	15	5	52	10	87
25	17	6	61	11	96
Months: 1	19	7	67	12	100
2	27				

BODILY INJURY

Class	15/30	20/40	20/50	25/50	25/60	50/100	100/300	250/500	500/1000
10	27	37	40	44	47	69	94	144	187
17	37	52	58	63	69	104	146	228	298
18	33	46	50	55	60	89	124	193	251
20	41	59	65	72	78	119	168	263	344

LOAN AMORTIZATION TABLE (MONTHLY PAYMENT PER $1,000 TO PAY PRINCIPAL AND INTEREST ON INSTALLMENT LOAN)

Terms in months	7.50%	8%	8.50%	9%	10.00%	10.50%	11.00%	11.50%	12.00%
6	$170.34	$170.58	$170.83	$171.20	$171.56	$171.81	$172.05	$172.30	$172.55
12	86.76	86.99	87.22	87.46	87.92	88.15	88.38	88.62	88.85
18	58.92	59.15	59.37	59.60	60.06	60.29	60.52	60.75	60.98
24	45.00	45.23	45.46	45.69	46.14	46.38	46.61	46.84	47.07
30	36.66	36.89	37.12	37.35	37.81	38.04	38.28	38.51	38.75
36	31.11	31.34	31.57	31.80	32.27	32.50	32.74	32.98	33.21
42	27.15	27.38	27.62	27.85	28.32	28.55	28.79	29.03	29.28
48	24.18	24.42	24.65	24.77	25.36	25.60	25.85	26.09	26.33
54	21.88	22.12	22.36	22.59	23.07	23.32	23.56	23.81	24.06
60	20.04	20.28	20.52	20.76	21.25	21.49	21.74	21.99	22.24

Terms in months	12.50%	13.00%	13.50%	14.00%	14.50%	15.00%	15.50%	16.00%
6	$172.80	$173.04	$173.29	$173.54	$173.79	$174.03	$174.28	$174.53
12	89.08	89.32	89.55	89.79	90.02	90.26	90.49	90.73
18	61.21	61.45	61.68	61.92	62.15	62.38	62.62	62.86
24	47.31	47.54	47.78	48.01	48.25	48.49	48.72	48.96
30	38.98	39.22	39.46	39.70	39.94	40.18	40.42	40.66
36	33.45	33.69	33.94	34.18	34.42	34.67	34.91	35.16
42	29.52	29.76	30.01	30.25	30.50	30.75	31.00	31.25
48	26.58	26.83	27.08	27.33	27.58	27.83	28.08	28.34
54	24.31	24.56	24.81	25.06	25.32	25.58	25.84	26.10
60	22.50	22.75	23.01	23.27	23.53	23.79	24.05	24.32

COLLISION

Classes	Age group	Symbols 1–3 $300 ded.	Symbol 4 $300 ded.	Symbol 5 $300 ded.	Symbol 6 $300 ded.	Symbol 7 $300 ded.	Symbol 8 $300 ded.	Symbol 10 $300 ded.
10–20	1	180	180	187	194	214	264	279
	2	160	160	166	172	190	233	246
	3	148	148	154	166	183	221	233
	4	136	136	142	160	176	208	221
	5	124	124	130	154	169	196	208

| | Additional cost to reduce deductible | |
Class	From $300 to $200	From $300 to $100
10	13	27
17	20	43
18	16	33
20	26	55

COMPREHENSIVE

Classes	Age group	Symbols 1–3 $300 ded.	Symbol 4 $300 ded.	Symbol 5 $300 ded.	Symbol 6 $300 ded.	Symbol 7 $300 ded.	Symbol 8 $300 ded.	Symbol 10 $300 ded.
10–25	1	61	61	65	85	123	157	211
	2	55	55	58	75	108	138	185
	3	52	52	55	73	104	131	178
	4	49	49	52	70	99	124	170
	5	47	47	49	67	94	116	163

Additional cost to reduce deductible: From $300 to $200 add $4

AMORTIZATION CHART (MORTGAGE PRINCIPAL AND INTEREST PER THOUSAND DOLLARS)

Term in years	7%	7½%	8%	8½%	9%	9½%	10%	10½%	11%	11½%	11¾%	12%
10	11.62	11.88	12.14	12.40	12.67	12.94	13.22	13.50	13.78	14.06	14.21	14.35
12	10.29	10.56	10.83	11.11	11.39	11.67	11.96	12.25	12.54	12.84	12.99	13.14
15	8.99	9.28	9.56	9.85	10.15	10.45	10.75	11.06	11.37	11.69	11.85	12.01
17	8.40	8.69	8.99	9.29	9.59	9.90	10.22	10.54	10.86	11.19	11.35	11.52
20	7.76	8.06	8.37	8.68	9.00	9.33	9.66	9.99	10.33	10.67	10.84	11.02
22	7.44	7.75	8.07	8.39	8.72	9.05	9.39	9.73	10.08	10.43	10.61	10.78
25	7.07	7.39	7.72	8.06	8.40	8.74	9.09	9.45	9.81	10.17	10.35	10.54
30	6.66	7.00	7.34	7.69	8.05	8.41	8.78	9.15	9.53	9.91	10.10	10.29
35	6.39	6.75	7.11	7.47	7.84	8.22	8.60	8.99	9.37	9.77	9.96	10.16

Term in years	12½%	12¾%	13%	13½%	13¾%	14%	14½%	14¾%	15%	15½%	16%
10	14.64	14.79	14.94	15.23	15.38	15.53	15.83	15.99	16.14	16.45	16.76
12	13.44	13.60	13.75	14.06	14.22	14.38	14.69	14.85	15.01	15.34	15.66
15	12.33	12.49	12.66	12.99	13.15	13.32	13.66	13.83	14.00	14.34	14.69
17	11.85	12.02	12.19	12.53	12.71	12.88	13.23	13.41	13.58	13.94	14.30
20	11.37	11.54	11.72	12.08	12.26	12.44	12.80	12.99	13.17	13.54	13.92
22	11.14	11.33	11.51	11.87	12.06	12.24	12.62	12.81	12.99	13.37	13.75
25	10.91	11.10	11.28	11.66	11.85	12.04	12.43	12.62	12.81	13.20	13.59
30	10.68	10.87	11.07	11.46	11.66	11.85	12.25	12.45	12.65	13.05	13.45
35	10.56	10.76	10.96	11.36	11.56	11.76	12.17	12.37	12.57	12.98	13.39

CHAPTER 1

Self-Paced Worksheet

Cover the answers on the right and fill in each blank. After answering the question, look to the right for your answer.

Vocabulary Review

1. The _____ _____ place-value chart divides groups of three digits right to left by units, thousands, millions, billions, and trillions.

2. The total in the adding process is called the _____.

3. The smaller number that is being subtracted from another is called the _____.

4. The answer from a subtraction problem is the _____.

5. Numbers that are combined in the addition process are called _____.

6. Multiplicand times multiplier equals the _____.

7. The _____ is the number in the division process that is dividing into another.

8. The _____ is the leftover amount in the division process.

9. _____ _____ _____ _____ results in only one nonzero digit left. This means rounding to first digit of number.

10. The _____ is the answer of a division problem.

1.	whole number
2.	sum
3.	subtrahend
4.	difference
5.	addends
6.	product
7.	divisor
8.	remainder
9.	rounding all the way
10.	quotient

Theory Tips (and/or Cautions)

11. The 5 in 7,853 is in the _____ place.

12. The 4 in 64,115,328 is in the _____ place.

13. In rounding 1,456 to the nearest thousands, the first step is to identify the _____ _____ of the digit you want to round.

14. In rounding, if digit to right of identified digit is _____ or greater, identified digit is increased by one.

15. Rounding all the way results in only _____ _____ digit remaining.

16. The first step in dissecting a word problem is to _____ _____ _____.

17. Adding of whole numbers is done _____ to _____.

18. The difference plus the subtrahend equals the _____.

19. The numbers between the multiplier and the product are _____ _____.

20. We can _____ the multiplication process by reversing the multiplicand and multiplier and then multiplying.

21. 75,000 × 20 is completed by multiplying 75 × 2 and _____ _____ zeros to answer.

22. The divisor times quotient plus remainder equals the _____.

23. 66,000 ÷ 100 results in dropping _____ zeros in the dividend.

11.	tens
12.	millions
13.	place value
14.	five
15.	one nonzero
16.	gather the facts
17.	top bottom
18.	minuend
19.	partial products
20.	check
21.	adding (affixing) four
22.	dividend
23.	two

Calculations/Applications

Do calculations on scrap paper as needed. Worked-out solutions are provided at end.

24. Write in verbal the whole number 8,593 and illustrate place values.

25. Round 9,852 to nearest hundred.

26. Round 62,555 to nearest thousand.

27. Round 6,853 all the way.

28. Estimate by rounding all the way and then do actual calculation.
    6,666
    7,500
    7,215

24.	eight thousand, five hundred ninety-three $(8 \times 1,000) + (5 \times 100) + (9 \times 10) + (3 \times 1)$
25.	9,900
26.	63,000
27.	7,000
28.	22,000 est. 21,381

29. Subtract: 9,432
                −3,618

30. Multiply 86 × 1,000 by the shortcut method.
31. Multiply 751 (do not multiply rows of zeros).
        406
32. Divide 7,041 ÷ 128 and show any remainder.
33. Divide 99,000 ÷ 100 by the shortcut method.
34. Chrysler produces 650 vans each workday (Monday through Friday). If the cost to produce each car is $7,000, what is Chrysler's cost for the year?

Worked-Out Solutions to Calculations/Applications Section

25. 9,852 → 9,900
        ↑

26. 62,555 → 63,000
         ↑

27. 6,853 → 7,000
        ↑

28. 6,666 → 7,000
    7,500 → 8,000
    7,215 → 7,000
    21,381   22,000

29. (8 14 2 12)
    9,432
    3,618
    5,814

30. 86 + 3 zeros

31.   751
         406
        4506
       30040
      304,906

32.   55 Rem1
      128)7041
          640
          641
          640
            1

33. 99,000 = 990

34.   5 × 650 = 3,250
       3,250 × 52 = 169,000
    169,000 × $7,000 = $1,183,000,000

Word Problem Practice Quiz

Check with your instructor for complete worked-out solutions.

1–1. Mel Jones received the following grades in a computer science class: 90, 70, 50, 85, 75, and 60. The instructor said he would drop the lowest grade. What is Mel's average?

1–2. Judy Small had a $850 balance in her checkbook. During the week, she wrote checks for rent, $180; telephone, $60; food, $95; and entertaining $45. She also made a deposit of $1,200. Calculate the new checkbook balance.

1–3. James Company carpeted its offices requiring 711 square yards of commercial carpet. The total cost of the carpet was $3,555. How much did James pay per square yard?

1–4. The Angel Company produced 26,580 cans of paint in August. Angel was able to sell 21,946 of these cans. Calculate ending inventory of paint cans along with its total inventory cost assuming each can cost $12.

1–5. A computer with a regular price of $4,500 was reduced by $1,255. Calculate the new selling price of the computer. Assuming 900 customers purchased the computer, what were the sales to the store?

1–6. Mills Hardware on Monday sold 40 rakes at $7 each, 8 wrenches at $5 each, 10 bags of grass seed at $6 each, 9 lawn mowers at $205 each, and 33 cans of paint at $4 each. What were the total dollar sales for Mills on Monday?

1–7. Dick Herch, a college editor, was going on a business trip that would take him from Boston (starting point) to New York and to Washington, D.C. Dick estimated he would be traveling 1,901 miles round trip. In actuality, the drive from Boston to New York was 228 miles, and from New York to Washington, D.C. was 242 miles. Calculate how many miles Dick overestimated his trip.

1–8. Jay Miller loves to ski. He rents a ski chalet for $1,350 per month for 4 months. What is Jay's rental charge for the 4 months? Assume Jay spends $6,250 for the total trip. How much did he spend above the renting of the ski chalet?

1–9. Jill Rite borrowed $20,000 to buy a new car. Assume a finance charge of $4,900. What will be her monthly payment if she takes 60 months to repay the loan (plus finance charge)? Assume the loan is repaid in equal payments.

1–10. Jim Rose bought 7,000 shares of stock in the Flight Company. After holding the stock for 6 months, he sold 400 shares on Monday, 330 shares on Tuesday and again on Thursday, and 800 shares on Friday. Calculate the total number of shares Jim still has. If the average share of stock is worth $39 per share, what is the total value of his stock?

CHAPTER 2

Self-Paced Worksheet

Cover the answers on the right and fill in each blank. After answering the question, look to the right for your answer.

Vocabulary Review

1. Like fractions are _____ _____ with the same denominators.
2. _____ is the reducing process to simplify multiplication and division of fractions.
3. A fraction reaches its _____ _____ when no number divides evenly into the numerator and denominator except the number 1.
4. $\frac{7}{5}$, of which 5 is called the _____.
5. A _____ _____ (larger than 1) is only divisible by itself and one.
6. The _____ _____ _____ is the smallest nonzero whole number into which all denominators will divide evenly.
7. The _____ _____ _____ is the largest possible number that will divide evenly into both the numerator and denominator.
8. The _____ of a fraction is the interchanging of the numerator and denominator.
9. An _____ _____ is when the numerator is equal to or greater than the denominator.
10. _____ _____ are proper fractions with different denominators.

1.	proper fractions
2.	cancellation
3.	lowest terms
4.	denominator
5.	prime number
6.	least common denominator
7.	greatest common divisor
8.	reciprocal
9.	improper fraction
10.	unlike fractions

Theory Tips (and/or Cautions)

11. When converting an improper fraction to a mixed number, the remainder will be placed over the _____ denominator.
12. When converting mixed numbers to improper fractions, the _____ will stay the same.
13. The greatest common divisor cannot be a _____.
14. Dividing numerator and denominator by the greatest common divisor will result in reducing the fraction to its _____ _____.
15. The _____ _____ you use is the greatest common divisor when using the step approach.
16. $\frac{2}{7}$ or $\frac{8}{28}$ are _____ in value.
17. In adding or subtracting fractions, they should be _____ _____ _____ terms.
18. In adding or subtracting fractions with different denominators, the _____ _____ _____ must be found.
19. In finding the LCD by prime numbers, the next highest prime number will be used if smaller prime number will not divide evenly into at least _____ numbers.
20. When borrowing _____ from a whole number where subtracting in a mixed number problem, it has the same value as $\frac{5}{5}$ or $\frac{4}{4}$.
21. $\frac{4}{1}$ is equal to _____.
22. If cancellation is not used in the multiplying of mixed numbers the answer may have to be _____ _____ _____ _____.
23. 5 and $\frac{1}{5}$ are _____. When these two numbers are multiplied, they equal 1.
24. If your answer is an _____ _____ be sure to reduce it to lowest terms.

11.	old
12.	denominator
13.	zero
14.	lowest terms
15.	last divisor
16.	equivalent
17.	reduced to lowest
18.	least common denominator
19.	two
20.	1
21.	4
22.	reduced to lowest terms
23.	reciprocals
24.	improper fraction

Calculations/Applications

Do calculations on scrap paper as needed. Worked-out solutions are provided at end.

25. Convert to mixed number: $\frac{150}{7}$
26. Convert to an improper fraction: $9\frac{5}{8}$
27. Find the GCD by step approach and reduce to lowest terms: $\frac{15}{80}$
28. Convert to higher terms: $\frac{7}{10} = \frac{}{90}$

25.	$21\frac{3}{7}$
26.	$\frac{77}{8}$
27.	$5; \frac{3}{16}$
28.	$\frac{63}{90}$

29. Find the LCD: 15 6 3 4 2

30. Subtract: $8\frac{1}{8} - 6\frac{7}{24}$

31. Multiply (use cancelling): $14 \times \frac{2}{7}$

32. Multiply (do not use cancelling; reduce by GCD): $\frac{7}{8} \times \frac{6}{9}$

33. Complete: $\frac{1}{4} \div \frac{3}{6}$

34. A recent testing survey showed $\frac{1}{4}$ of all people surveyed preferred baking soda toothpaste to regular. If 26,000 people were in the survey, how many favored regular toothpaste? How many favored baking soda toothpaste?

Worked-Out Solutions to Calculations/Applications Section

25.
$$7\overline{)150} = 21\frac{3}{7}$$
$$\frac{14}{10}$$
$$\frac{7}{3}$$

26. $9\frac{5}{8} = \frac{72+5}{8} = \frac{77}{8}$

27.
$$15\overline{)80} \qquad \textcircled{5}\,\overline{)15} \qquad \frac{15 \div 5}{80 \div 5} = \frac{3}{16}$$
$$\frac{75}{5} \qquad \frac{15}{}$$
(quotients: 5 and 3)

28. $\frac{7}{10} = \frac{63}{90} \leftarrow (9 \times 7)$

29.
$$2\,\lfloor 15 \quad 6 \quad 3 \quad 4 \quad 2$$
$$3\,\lfloor 15 \quad 3 \quad 3 \quad 2 \quad 1$$
$$5 \quad 1 \quad 1 \quad 2 \quad 1$$

$2 \times 3 \times 5 \times 1 \times 1 \times 2 \times 1 = 60$

30.
$$8\frac{1}{8} = 8\frac{3}{24} = 7\frac{27}{24}$$
$$-6\frac{7}{24} - 6\frac{7}{24} = 6\frac{7}{24}$$
$$= 1\frac{20}{24} = 1\frac{5}{6}$$

31. $\overset{2}{14} \times \frac{2}{7} = 4$ (denominator 1)

32. $\frac{7}{8} \times \frac{6}{9} = \frac{42}{72}$
$$42\overline{)72} \qquad 30\overline{)42} \qquad 12\overline{)30} \qquad 6\overline{)12}$$
$$\frac{42}{30} \qquad \frac{30}{12} \qquad \frac{24}{6} \qquad \frac{12}{}$$
(quotients: 1, 1, 2, 2)
$$\frac{42 \div 6}{72 \div 6} = \frac{7}{12}$$

33. $\frac{1}{4} \times \frac{\overset{3}{\cancel{6}}}{\cancel{3}} = \frac{1}{2}$

34. $\frac{3}{4} \times 26{,}000 = 19{,}500$
$$\frac{1}{4} \times 26{,}000 = 6{,}500$$

Word Problem Practice Quiz

Check with your instructor for complete worked-out solutions.

2–1. A survey conducted by a marketing class found that $\frac{7}{8}$ of all people surveyed favored digital watches over traditional styles. If 3,200 responded to the survey, how many actually favored using traditional watches?

2–2. Jack, Alice, and Frank entered into a partnership. Jack owns $\frac{1}{5}$ of the company and Alice owns $\frac{1}{8}$. Calculate what part is owned by Frank.

2–3. Bob Campbell, who loves to cook, makes an apple pie (serves 6) for his family. The recipe calls for $3\frac{1}{2}$ cups of apples, $2\frac{3}{4}$ cups of flour, $\frac{1}{8}$ cup of margarine, $2\frac{1}{8}$ cups of sugar, and 5 eggs. Since guests are coming, he would like to make this pie to serve 24. How much of each ingredient should Bob use?

2–4. A trip from Boston to the White Mountains of New Hampshire will take $2\frac{7}{8}$ hours. Assume we are $\frac{1}{7}$ of the way there. How much longer will the trip take?

2–5. The price of a new van has increased by $\frac{2}{5}$. If the original price of the van was $15,000, what is the new price today?

2–6. Jim Smith felled a tree that was 120 feet long. Jim decided to cut the tree into pieces of $2\frac{1}{2}$ feet. How many pieces can be cut from this tree?

2–7. JHS Company's stock on Monday reached a high of $\$99\frac{1}{8}$ per share. At the end of the day the stock plummeted to $\$68\frac{5}{8}$. How much did the stock fall from its high on Monday?

2–8. During the winter, Bill Blank has been quite concerned about the total number of gallons of home heating fuel he used. Last winter he used $1{,}505\frac{7}{8}$ gallons of oil. Here is a summary of this year's usage. Is it more or less than the previous year? Also, how much more or less?

December	$525\frac{1}{4}$	February	$481\frac{3}{8}$
January	$488\frac{5}{8}$	March	$255\frac{1}{3}$

2–9. John Toby is paid $70 per day. John became ill on Monday and had to leave after $\frac{3}{7}$ of a day. What did he earn on Monday? (Assume no work, no pay).

2–10. Evan Summers bought $1\frac{3}{8}$ pounds of roast beef, $4\frac{5}{7}$ pounds of sliced cheese, and $\frac{3}{5}$ of a pound of coleslaw. What is the total weight of his purchases?

CHAPTER 3

Self-Paced Worksheet

Cover the answers on the right and fill in each blank. After answering the question, look to the right for your answer.

Vocabulary Review

1. The position located between units and tenths is called the _____ _____.
2. _____ are numbers written with digits to right of the decimal point.
3. A _____ _____ is a fraction with a denominator that has a power of 10.
4. A _____ _____ has no whole number(s) to left of the decimal point.
5. A _____ _____ is a combination of a whole number and a decimal.
6. Decimal numbers that repeat themselves continuously are called _____ _____.

1. decimal point
2. decimals
3. decimal fraction
4. pure decimal
5. mixed decimal
6. repeating decimals

Theory Tips (and/or Cautions)

7. 4.53918   The 1 is in the _____ _____ place value.
8. In rounding decimals, drop _____ _____ to right of the identified digit.
9. .8, .80, .800 all have the same _____.
10. .33$\overline{3}$ is an example of a _____ decimal.
11. 3.0, 3.000, 3.0000 all have the same _____.
12. If the total number of places is greater than there are places in the product (from multiplying decimals), insert _____ in front of the product.
13. The _____ does not change when we multiply the divisor and dividend by the same number.
14. When multiplying decimals by multiples of 10, the answers are _____ than the original number.
15. When dividing decimals by multiples of 10, the answers are _____ than the original number.

7. ten thousandths
8. all digits
9. value
10. repeating
11. value
12. zeros
13 quotient
14. larger
15. smaller

Calculations/Applications

Do calculations on scrap paper as needed. Worked-out solutions are provided at end.

16. .3333 rounded to nearest thousandths is _____.
17. .16593 rounded to nearest hundredth is _____.
18. Convert to a decimal: $\frac{88}{100,000}$
19. .713 converted to a decimal fraction is _____.
20. .07$\frac{1}{4}$ converted to a decimal fraction is _____.
21. $\frac{1}{6}$ converted to decimal is _____ (round to nearest hundredth).
22. Rearrange vertically and add: 4.1, 14.82, 16.321
23. Multiply and round to nearest hundredth: 15.41 × 18.8
24. Divide and round to nearest hundredth: 3,142 ÷ 3.91
25. Complete by shortcut method: 4,138 ÷ 10,000
26. At Hertz, the cost per day to rent a full-size car is $49.99, plus $.18 per mile. What is the charge to rent this car for 2 days if you drove 959.8 miles?
27. A $2,800 computer would cost how much in Canada? (Use table in *Business Math Handbook*; round to nearest cent.)

16. .333
17. .17
18. .00088
19. $\frac{713}{1,000}$
20. $\frac{725}{10,000}$
21. .17
22. 35.241
23. 289.71
24. 803.58
25. .4138
26. $272.74
27. $3,814.72

Worked-Out Solutions to Calculations/Applications Section

16. .33$\underset{\uparrow}{3}$3 → .333

17. .16$\underset{\uparrow}{5}$93 → .17

18. $\dfrac{88}{100,000}$ $\begin{array}{l}\leftarrow .00088 \\ 5 \text{ places}\end{array}$

19. $\dfrac{713}{1,000}$ (1 + 3 places)

20. $.07\frac{1}{4} \rightarrow$
$$
\begin{array}{r}
.07 \\
+.0025 \\
\hline
.0725 \rightarrow \dfrac{725}{1+4\text{ places}} = \dfrac{725}{10{,}000}
\end{array}
$$

21. $\dfrac{1}{6} = .16\overset{\uparrow}{6} = .17$

22.
$$
\begin{array}{r}
4.100 \\
14.820 \\
16.321 \\
\hline
35.241
\end{array}
$$

23.
$$
\begin{array}{r}
15.41 \\
\times\ 18.8 \\
\hline
12328 \\
12328 \\
1541 \\
\hline
289708 \rightarrow 289.708 \rightarrow 289.71
\end{array}
$$

24.
$$
\begin{array}{r}
803.580 \\
3.91\,)\overline{314200.000} \rightarrow 803.58 \\
3128 \\
\hline
1400 \\
1173 \\
\hline
2270 \\
1955 \\
\hline
3150 \\
3128 \\
\hline
220
\end{array}
$$

25. $.4138 \rightarrow .4138$

26.
$$
\begin{array}{r}
\$49.99 \times 2 = \$\ 99.98 \\
\$.18 \times 959.8 = \underline{172.76} \\
\text{Total charge} = \$272.74
\end{array}
$$

27. $\$2{,}800 \times \$1.3624 = \$3{,}814.72$

Word Problem Practice Quiz

Check with your instructor for complete worked-out solutions.
Round where applicable to nearest hundredth.

3–1. Bob Baker bought season tickets to a professional basketball team's games. The cost was $795.88. The package included 38 home games. What is the average price of the tickets per game? Round to nearest cent. Jim has requested to buy 4 of the tickets from Bob. What will be the total price Bob should receive?

3–2. The level of the oil tank in Henry's basement at the beginning of January read 310.75 gallons. During the month it was filled with 112.85 gallons. Henry used 125.95 gallons in January. What is the number of gallons of oil that Henry has to begin February?

3–3. Printed pencils cost $.08\overline{3}$ each for an order of 144,000 pencils. On Monday, Jim Company placed an order for the 144,000 pencils. What is the cost of the pencils for Jim Company? (Hint: Use the fractional equivalent in your calculation.)

3–4. Irene was shopping for corn beef at Market A; it was $2.158 per pound. At Market B, corn beef was $2.06 per pound. How much cheaper is Market B?

3–5. Shelley Scupper bought a new sweater for $101.88. She gave the salesperson two $100 bills. what is Shelley's change?

3–6. Joe is traveling to a convention by car. His company will reimburse him $.34 per mile. Assume Joe traveled 1,011.8 miles. What reimbursement can he expect?

3–7. Morris Katz bought 4 new tires for his car at $129.35 per tire. He was also charged $3.15 per tire for mounting, $2.80 per tire for valve cores, and $4.95 per tire for balancing. Assuming no tax, what did Morris really pay for those 4 tires?

3–8. Alice wants to put wall-to-wall carpeting in her house. She will need 108.7 yards for downstairs, 19.8 yards for halls, and 175.9 yards for the upstairs bedrooms. She chose a shag carpet that costs $14.95 per yard. Alice also ordered foam padding at $3.25 per year. The installers quoted Alice a labor cost of $6.10 per yard in installation. What will the total job cost Alice?

3–9. A trip to Mexico costs 4,900 pesos. How much would this be in U.S. dollars? Check your answer.

3–10. The normal winter snowfall is 129.55 inches for Jordan County. this winter, the following snowfall resulted:

	Inches
December	29.33
January	44.453
February	18.85
March	16.35

What was this winter's total snowfall? How much was the snowfall above or below normal?

CHAPTER 4

Self-Paced Worksheet

Cover the answers on the right and fill in each blank. After answering the question, look to the right for your answer.

Vocabulary Review:

1. _____ _____ is the process of comparing the bank balance to the checkbook balance.

2. A record-keeping device called a _____ _____ records checks paid and deposits made by companies using a checking account.

3. A _____ _____ provides a record of checks written.

4. A _____ _____ identifies the next person or company to whom the check is to be transferred.

5. The _____ is the one who is named to receive the amount of the check.

6. Credit card sales less returns equal _____ _____.

7. A _____ memo indicates what a bank is adding to your account.

8. One who writes the check is called the _____.

9. _____ _____ _____ are deposits not received or processed by the bank at the time the bank statement is prepared.

10. Checks written but not yet processed by the bank before the bank statement preparation are called _____ _____.

Theory Tips (and/or Cautions)

11. If the verbal amount on a check doesn't match the figure amount, the bank by law uses the _____ amount.

12. _____ _____ can be further endorsed by someone who receives it intentionally or through loss.

13. A _____ _____ means the bank is decreasing one's account.

14. _____ is an important cause of differences between bank and checkbook.

15. An NSF will result in the bank _____ one's checkbook balance.

16. In the reconciliation process, deposits in transit and outstanding checks affect the _____ balance.

17. If the bank statement shows a note collected, the checkbook balance in the reconciliation process will be _____.

18. If a $20 check was recorded as $10, we need to lower the _____ balance by another $10.

19. Interest earned on a checking account will be _____ to one's account.

20. ATM cards are _____ cards.

21. Check stubs should be _____ before the check is written.

1.	bank reconciliation
2.	check register
3.	check stub
4.	full endorsement
5.	payee
6.	net deposits
7.	credit
8.	drawer
9.	deposits in transit
10.	outstanding checks
11.	verbal
12.	blank endorsement
13.	debit memorandum
14.	timing
15.	lowering
16.	bank
17.	increased
18.	checkbook
19.	credited
20.	debit
21.	completed

Calculations/Applications

Do calculations on scrap paper as needed. Worked-out solutions are provided at end.

22. Given the following from the check register, calculate the ending balance.

Beginning balance	$481.92
Payment	$ 81.22
Payment	19.44
Deposit	111.22
Payment	88.04

22. $404.44

23. Calculate the net deposit from the following:

Credit card sales	Credit card returns
$ 15.88	$ 12.88
108.44	142.80
339.40	

23. $308.04

24. Write the following amount in verbal form as you would on a check: $675.88

24. Six hundred seventy-five and 88/100

25. Calculate reconciled bank balance, given the following:

Bank statement balance	$4,800.10
Checks outstanding	55.32
Deposits in transit	105.99

25. $4,850.77

26. Calculate reconciled checkbook balance, given the following:

Checkbook balance	$4,511.20
Interest earned	15.10
Note collected	555.10
ATM withdrawal	66.90
NSF check	12.55

26. $5,001.95

27. Calculate a reconciled balance from the following:

Checkbook balance	$2,885
Bank balance	2,999
Interest earned	22
Deposits in transit	500
Checks outstanding	620
NSF check	15
Check printing	13

27. $2,879

28. Angel's checkbook balance was $9,000. The bank statement had a balance of $10,500. Angel's bookkeeper noticed checks No. 140 for $550 and No. 145 for $205 were not yet processed by the bank. Angel made a deposit of $1,200 that had not reached the bank before preparation of the bank statement. Bank service charges totaled $40. The statement showed that the bank collected a note from Angel for $2,020 charging a $20 collection fee. Angel's bookkeeper noticed that a check for $30 was recorded as $15. What is the reconciled balance?

28. $10,945

Worked-Out Solutions to Calculations/Applications Section

22. $481.92 − $81.22 − $19.44 + $111.22 − $88.04 = $404.44

23.

$ 15.88		**25.** $4,800.10 − $55.32 + $105.99 = $4,850.77
108.44	$463.72	
+ 339.40	− 155.68 ($12.88 + $142.80)	
$463.72	$308.04	

26.

$4,511.20		**27.**	$2,885	
+ 15.10			+ 22	$2,999
+ 555.10			− 15	+ 500
− 66.90			− 13	− 620
− 12.55			$2,879	$2,879
$5,001.95				

28.

Checkbook		Bank	
Angel's checkbook balance	$ 9,000	Bank balance	$10,500
Add:		Add:	
Collection of note (less fee)	2,000	Deposits in transit	1,200
	$11,000		$11,700
Deduct:		Deduct:	
		Outstanding checks:	
Bank service charge: $40		No. 140 $550	
Book error 15	55	No. 145 205	755
Reconciled balance	$10,945	Reconciled balance	$10,945

Word Problem Practice Quiz

Check with your instructor for complete worked-out solutions.

4–1. Jones Bank sent a bank statement to Venice Company showing an ending balance of $1,900.00. There was a service charge of $9.00 on the bank statement. The bookkeeper of Venice Company noticed in the reconciliation process a deposit in transit of $850 along with checks outstanding of $300. Complete the reconciliation for Venice assuming a beginning balance of $2,459.

4–2. Al Ring received his bank statement from Jones Bank indicating a balance of $1,751.88. Ring's checkbook showed a balance of $1,512.70. Al noticed that a check for $261.18 was outstanding. The bank statement also revealed a NSF check for $12.00 and a service charge of $10.00. Reconcile this bank statement for Al.

4–3. The Bank statement for Janet Company revealed a balance of $2,585.22, while the checkbook balance showed $2,345.84. Checks for $116.55 and $129.33 were outstanding. A check printing charge for $6.50 was on the bank statement. Prepare a bank reconciliation.

4–4. The checkbook balance of Jeep Company showed a balance of $10,636.15. The bank statement showed a balance of $9,750.44. Checks outstanding totaled $2,850.11. There was a deposit in transit of $3,525.32 along with a NSF notice for $225.00. Jeep Company had earned interest of $14.50 of its checking account. Prepare a bank reconciliation.

4–5. On May 29, 1997, Lou Co. had the following MasterCard transactions (along with some returns)—Sales: $55.10, $16.92, $101.55; Return: $6.99, $18.11. Calculate the total net deposits.

4–6. The checkbook of Moore Company showed a balance of $5,844.61. The bank statement revealed a balance of $6,950.11. Check Nos. 59 and 68 were outstanding for $750 and $219, respectively. A deposit for $435 was not listed on the bank statement. The bank collected a $600 note for Moore. Check charges for the month were $28.50. Prepare a bank reconciliation.

4–7. The checkbook balance of Roe Company is $7,069.77. The bank statement reveals a balance of $3,940.11. The bank statement showed interest earned of $24, and a service charge of $15.10. There is a deposit in transit of $6,850.44. Outstanding checks totaled $1,911.88. The bookkeeper in further analyzing the bank statement noticed a collection of a note by bank for $3,000. Roe Company forgot to deduct a check for $1,200 during the month. Prepare a bank reconciliation.

4–8. The bank statement of May 31 for Jay Company showed a balance of $6,600.11. The bookkeeper of Jay Company noticed from the bank statement that the bank had collected a note for $1,500.00. There was a deposit in transit that Jay Company made on June 1 for $5,008.10, along with the outstanding checks of $2,210.11. Check charges were $52.00. Assist the bookkeeper of Jay in preparing a reconciled statement. Assume the checkbook balance of Jay equals to $7,950.10.

4–9. On December 31, the checkbook balance of Rose Company was $8,437.00. The bank statement balance showed $9,151.88. Checks outstanding totaled $1,341.88. The statement revealed a deposit in transit of $610.55, as well as a check charge of $11.80. The company earned interest income of $7.50 that was shown on the report. The bookkeeper forgot to record a check for $12.15. Complete a bank reconciliation for Rose.

4–10. Skol's checkbook currently has a balance of $12,280.56. The bank statement shows a balance of $8,915.33. The statement revealed interest income of $27.00, along with check charges of $18.10. Skol recorded a $115 check as $100. Deposits in transit were $5,811.44. Check Nos. 85, 88, and 92 for $800.11, $700.88, and $951.32 were not returned with the statement. Prepare a bank reconciliation for Skol.

CHAPTER 5

Self-Paced Worksheet

Cover the answers on the right and fill in each blank. After answering the question, look to the right for your answer.

Vocabulary Review

1. A number such as 4 or −8 is called a _____.
2. An _____ is a math statement that shows equality for expressions or numbers or both.
3. _____ numbers are a collection of numbers with negative signs.
4. _____ numbers are a collection of numbers with a positive sign.
5. The variable we are solving for is called an _____.
6. _____ are letters or symbols that represent unknowns.

Theory Tips (and/or Cautions)

7. The letter _____ could be a variable or confused with multiplication.
8. Constants have a _____ value.
9. If a variable has no number in front of it, it is assumed to be _____.
10. $A \times B$; $A \cdot B$; $A(B)$ all mean A _____ B.
11. The sum of two positive numbers is _____.
12. The sum of two negative numbers is _____.
13. Positive minus a negative means _____.
14. If the equation process is addition, solve for the unknown by _____.
15. You do not _____ or divide an equation by zero.
16. When solving for an unknown that involves more than one step, do _____ and _____ before multiplication and division.
17. If an equation contains parenthesis, first multiply _____ _____ inside the parenthesis by the number or letter outside the parenthesis.

Calculations/Applications

Do calculations on scrap paper as needed. Worked-out solutions are provided at end.

18. $P - \$40 = \$70$. $P =$ _____.
19. $\frac{1}{7}V = 900$. $V =$ _____.
20. $5C - C = 100$. $C =$ _____.
    $5C =$ _____.
21. $5W + 2(10 - W) = 50$. $W =$ _____.
22. Situation 5 in LU 5–2 is when total units _____ _____ _____ and know which sells better.
23. Situation 6 in LU 5–2 is when total units _____ _____ and don't know which sells best.
24. A pair of Reebok sneakers was reduced $40. The sale price was $90. The original price was _____.
25. A local KFC restaurant budgets $\frac{1}{12}$ of its monthly profits on salaries. Salaries for the month were $6,000. The monthly profit for KFC was _____.
26. Lowell Co. sold 6 times as many lamps as Ryan Co. The difference in their sales is 125. Lowell sold _____ lamps.
27. Al and Pete sold 400 homes for Century 21 Real Estate. Al sold seven times as many homes as Pete. Al sold _____ homes.
28. On Monday, Smith Co. sold $350 worth of calculators ($12) and watches ($10). Customers bought 5 times as many calculators as watches. How many calculators and watches did Smith sell on Monday?

1.	constant
2.	equation
3.	negative
4.	positive
5.	unknown
6.	variables
7.	X
8.	fixed
9.	one
10.	times
11.	positive
12.	negative
13.	adding
14.	subtraction
15.	multiply
16.	addition; subtraction
17.	each item
18.	$110
19.	6,300
20.	$C = 25$ $5C = 125$
21.	$W = 10$
22.	are not given
23.	are given
24.	$130
25.	$72,000
26.	150
27.	350
28.	25 calculators; 5 watches

29. On Monday, Smith Co. sold calculators ($12) and watches ($10). A total of 30 sales of watches and calculators were $350. How many of each did Smith sell?

Worked-Out Solutions to Calculations/Applications Section

18.
$$P - \$40 = \$\ 70$$
$$\underline{+\ 40 = +\ 40}$$
$$P \qquad = \$110$$

19.
$$\frac{1}{7}V = \ 900$$
$$7\left(\frac{1}{7}V\right) = \ 900\ (7)$$
$$V = 6{,}300$$

20.
$$5C - C = 100$$
$$\frac{4C}{4} = \frac{100}{4}$$
$$C = 25$$
$$5C = 125$$

21.
$$5W + 20 - 2W = \ 50$$
$$3W + 20 = \ 50$$
$$\underline{-20 = -20}$$
$$\frac{3W}{3} = \frac{30}{3}$$
$$W = 10$$

24.
$$P - \$40 = \$\ 90$$
$$\underline{+\ 40 \quad +\ 40}$$
$$P \qquad = \$130$$

25.
$$\frac{1}{12}P = \$6{,}000$$
$$12\left(\frac{1}{12}\right)P = \$6{,}000\ (12)$$
$$P = \$72{,}000$$

26.
$$6L - L = 125$$
$$\frac{5L}{5} = \frac{125}{5}$$
$$L = 25 \qquad 25 \times 6 = 150$$

27.
$$7H + H = 400$$
$$\frac{8H}{8} = \frac{400}{8}$$
$$H = 50 \qquad 7 \times 50 = 350$$

28.

Calculators	5W	$12	60W
Watches	W*	10	+ 10W
			$350

$$60W + 10W = 350 \qquad \text{25 calculators}$$
$$\frac{70W}{70} = \frac{350}{70} \qquad \text{5 watches}$$
$$W = 5$$

For Situation 5, assign variable to one that sells the least.

29.

Calculators	C*	$12	12C
Watches	30 − C	10	+ 10 (30 − C)
			$350

$$12C + 10(30 - C) = \ 350$$
$$12C + 300 - 10C = \ 350$$
$$2C + 300 = \ 350$$
$$\underline{-\ 300 = -\ 300}$$
$$\frac{2C}{2} = \frac{50}{2} \qquad \text{25 calculators}$$
$$C = 25 \qquad \text{5 watches}$$
$$(30 - 25) = 5$$

For Situation 6, assign variable to most expensive.

Word Problem Practice Quiz

Check with your instructor for complete worked-out solutions.

5–1. What number decreased by 605 equals 1,090?

5–2. One eighth of all sales at Al's Diner are for cash. If cash sales for the week were $1,250, what were Al's total sales?

5–3. Christina is 9 times Judith's age. If the difference in their age is 24, how old is each?

5–4. D. Darby and J. Jonathan sell cars for Jean's Auto. Over the past year they sold 290 cars. Assume Darby sells 4 times as many cars as Jonathan. How many cars did each sell?

5–5. The Computer Store sells diskettes ($3) and boxes of computer paper ($4). If total sales were $3,100 and customers bought 9 times as many diskettes as boxes of computer paper, what would be the number of each sold? Show proof that unit sales do equal the total dollar sales.

5–6. Pens cost $6 per carton, and rubber bands cost $4 per carton. If an order comes to a total of 70 cartons for $300, what was the specific number of cartons of pens as well as rubber bands? (Hint: Let P equal cartons of pens.)

5–7. Jim Murray and Phyllis Lowe received a total of $250,000 from a deceased relative's estate. They decided to put away $50,000 in a trust for their child and divide the remainder into $\frac{3}{4}$ for Phyllis and $\frac{1}{4}$ for Jim. How much will Phyllis and Jim receive?

5–8. In Ajax Corporation, the first shift produced $4\frac{1}{2}$ times as many lightbulbs as the second shift. If the number of lightbulbs produced was 55,000, how many lightbulbs were produced on each shift?

5–9. Jarvis Company sells thermometers ($4) and hot water bottles ($9). If total sales were $825 and customers bought 6 times as many thermometers as hot water bottles, what would be the number of each sold? Check that your result is equal to total dollar sales.

5–10. Wrenches cost $120 per carton and hammers cost $400 per carton. An order comes in for a total of 70 cartons for $15,400. How many cartons of wrenches and hammers are involved? Check your answer. (Hint: Let *H* equal hammers.)

CHAPTER 6

Self-Paced Worksheet

Cover the answers on the right and fill in each blank. After answering the question, look to the right for your answer.

Vocabulary Review

1. The _____ is the beginning whole quantity to which something is being compared.
2. The _____ is a percent, decimal, or fraction that indicates the part of the base you must calculate.
3. The _____ stands for hundredths.
4. The _____ is the amount or part that results from multiplying the base times the rate.
5. The _____ _____ is the decrease in price divided by the original amount.
6. The _____ _____ is the increase in price divided by the original amount.

1.	base
2.	rate
3.	percent
4	portion
5.	percent decrease
6.	percent increase

Theory Tips (and/or Cautions)

7. .008 means $\frac{8}{10}$ of _____ percent.
8. When a percent is less than 1%, the decimal conversion has at least _____ leading zeros before the whole number.
9. In rounding percents, digits to the right of the identified digit will be _____.
10. 22.5% is an example of a _____ percent.
11. In converting a mixed percent to a fraction first convert it to an _____ _____ before multiplying by 1/100.
12. The portion could be larger than the base if the rate is _____ than 100%.
13. The old year, or old price would be the _____.
14. In an increase or decrease problem, the difference in the price would be the _____.
15. The portion and rate will refer to the same part of the _____.
16. The base will be larger than the portion if the rate is _____ than 100%.
17. Portion = Base × _____.
18. The base represents _____ percent.
19. If sales are up to $4,000 a 20% increase in the new year and we are looking for sales in the old year the rate will be _____ percent of the old year.
20. The _____ is larger than the base if the rate is greater than 100%.

7.	one
8.	two
9.	deleted
10.	decimal
11.	improper fraction
12.	greater
13.	base
14.	portion
15.	base
16.	less
17.	rate
18.	100
19.	120%
20	portion

Calculations/Applications

Do calculations on scrap paper as needed. Worked-out solutions are provided at end.

21. .006 converted to a percent is _____.
22. $7\frac{3}{4}$% converted to a decimal is _____.
23. $\frac{17}{22}$ converted to a percent is _____ (round to the nearest hundredth percent).
24. $14\frac{1}{4}$% converted to a fraction is _____.
25. 11.4% converted to a fraction is _____.
26. Twelve out of 29 students in Professor Okimato's class received an "A" grade. What percent of the class did not receive the "A" grade? (Round to the nearest tenth percent.)
27. Computer City has yet to receive 70% of his computer order. Computer City received 90 computers to date. What was the original order?
28. In 1997, a local Pizza Hut shop had sales of $450,000. In 1998, sales were up 30%. What are the shop sales in 1998?
29. The price of a Saab 9000 increased in price from $24,500 to $29,000. What was the percent increase? (Round to the nearest hundredth percent.)

21.	.6%
22.	.0775
23.	77.27%
24.	$\frac{57}{400}$
25.	$\frac{57}{500}$
26.	58.6%
27.	300 computers
28.	$585,000
29.	18.37%

Worked-Out Solutions to Calculations/Applications Section

22. $7\% = .07$
$\dfrac{3}{4}\% = .0075$ $\Bigg\} = .0775$

23. $77.2727\% \rightarrow 77.27\%$
$\qquad\quad\uparrow$

24. $14\dfrac{1}{4}\% = \dfrac{57}{4} \times \dfrac{1}{100} = \dfrac{57}{400}$

25. $11.4\% \rightarrow 11\dfrac{4}{10}$
$\rightarrow \dfrac{114}{10} \times \dfrac{1}{100}$
$= \dfrac{114}{1{,}000}$
$= \dfrac{57}{500}$

26.

12 A's 29 students	Percent did not receive A	B: 29 R: ? P: 17 (29 − 12)	![circle diagram: P 17, B 29, R ?] $\dfrac{17}{29} = 58.62\%$ $= 58.6\%$

27.

70% of order not in 90 computers received	Original order	B: ? R: .30 (100% − 70%) P: 90	![circle diagram: P 90, B ?, R .30] $\dfrac{90}{.30} = 300$

Note: 90 computers is 30% of the total, not 70%.

28.

1997 $450,000 in sales 1998 Sales up 30%	Sales of 1998	B: $450,000 R: 1.30 (100% + 30%) P: ?	![circle diagram: P ?, $450,000 1.30, B R] $\begin{array}{r}\$450{,}000\\ \times\ 1.30\\ \hline \$585{,}000\end{array}$

Note: The Portion is larger than the Base since Rate is greater than 100%.

29.

$24,500 old price $29,000 new price	Percent increase	B: $24,500 (orig) R: ? P: $4,500 (diff. in price)	![circle diagram: P $4,500, B $24,500, R ?] $\dfrac{\$4{,}500}{\$24{,}500} = 18.367\% = 18.37\%$

Keep in mind:
a. The Portion and Rate must relate to same piece of the Base.
b. The Portion will be larger than the Base if the Rate is greater than 100%.

Word Problem Practice Quiz

Check with your instructor for complete worked-out solutions.

6–1. A stove increased in price from $650 to $1,280. What was the percent of increase? Round to the nearest hundredth percent.

6–2. The price of a calculator dropped from $38.95 to $17.49. What was the percent decrease in price? Round to nearest tenth percent.

6–3. Joan Smith bought an IBS Personal Computer priced at $1,688. She put down 40%. What is the amount of the down payment Joan made?

6–4. Earl Miller receives an annual salary of $50,000 from PB Stationery. Today his boss informs him that he will be getting a $4,700 raise. What percent of his old salary is the $4,700 raise? Round to nearest tenth percent.

6–5. Northwest Community College has 4,900 female students. This represents 70% of the total student body. How many students attend NW Community College?

6–6. At the Museum of Fine Arts it was estimated that 40% of all visitors are from in state. On Saturday, 7,000 people attended the museum. What is the number of out-of-state people in attendance?

6–7. Sharon Fox, insurance agent, earned a commission of $840 in her first week on the job. Her commission percent is 12%. What were Sharon's total sales for the week?

6–8. John's Bookstore ordered 500 business math texts. On verifying the order, only 80 books were actually received. What percent of the order was missing?

6–9. Joshua Wright was reviewing the total accounts receivable. This month he received $180,000 from credit customers. This represented 60% of all receivables due. What is the total amount of Joshua Wright's accounts receivable?

6–10. Veek Company in 1997 had sales of $950,000. In 1998, sales were up 66%. Calculate the sales for 1998.

CHAPTER 7

Self-Paced Worksheet

Cover the answers on the right and fill in each blank. After answering the question, look to the right for your answer.

Vocabulary Review

1. A _____ _____ is the result of making an early payment within the discount period.

2. _____ _____ is the list price less the amount of trade discount.

3. _____ _____ _____ rate is found by taking the complement of each term in the discount and multiplying them together. This rate shows the actual cost to the buyer for each dollar. This rate is not rounded.

4. 1 − Net price equivalent rate equals the _____ _____ _____ rate. This rate is not rounded.

5. A _____ _____ is two or more trade discounts that are applied to the balance remaining after the previous discount is taken.

6. The amount of time to take advantage of a cash discount is the _____ _____.

7. If the discount period is missed, payment is due by the end of the _____ _____.

8. _____ _____ means seller pays cost of freight to get goods to buyer's location.

9. _____ _____ _____ means buyer pays cost of freight to getting goods to his location.

10. _____ means the same as end of month.

11. The _____ _____ is the suggested retail price paid by customers.

12. The _____ is 100% less the stated percent.

1.	cash discount
2.	net price
3.	net price equivalent
4.	single equivalent discount
5.	chain discount
6.	discount period
7.	credit period
8.	FOB destination
9.	FOB shipping point
10.	proximo
11.	list price
12.	complement

Theory Tips (and/or Cautions)

13. Trade discounts may be _____ discounts or a _____ of discounts.

14. Trade discounts are not taken on _____, returned goods, or sales tax.

15. _____ _____ are never added together.

16. The _____ _____ _____ _____ is never rounded.

17. The _____ price times the net price equivalent rate is rounded to the nearest cent.

18. The _____ _____ _____ rate shows what the buyer saves per dollar.

19. _____ _____ should be taken before cash discounts.

20. Cash discounts are taken on the _____ _____.

21. FOB destination means the _____ pays the freight cost.

22. When using the exact days in a year calendar, if the two dates are in the same year you take the _____ between the table look-up number.

23. When using the exact days in a year calendar, if the two dates are in different years from the first year table look-up will have to be _____ from 365.

24. If credit terms are 2/10 EOM and purchase is on November 5, the _____ _____ ends on December 10.

25. If credit terms are 2/10 EOM and purchase is on April 29, the discount period ends on _____.

26. Partial payments are calculated by what you can afford. The partial payment is divided by one _____ the discount rate.

13.	single; chain
14.	freight
15.	chain discounts
16.	net price equivalent rate
17.	list
18.	single equivalent discount
19.	trade discounts
20.	net price
21.	seller
22.	difference
23.	subtracted
24.	discount period
25.	June 10
26.	minus

Calculations/Applications

Do calculations on scrap paper as needed. Worked-out solutions are provided at end.

27. A chain discount of 15/3/2 results in a net price equivalent rate of _____.

27.	.80801

28. The single equivalent discount rate in #27 would be _____.

29. A cellular phone had a list price of $250 with a chain discount of 8/6. Calculate the net price and trade discount amount.

30. Complete the following:

Invoice date	Date goods received	Terms	Last day of discount period	End of credit period
a. July 8		1/10,n/30	?	?
b. March 8		2/10 EOM	?	?
c. July 9	Oct. 4	3/10,n/30 ROG	?	?
d. March 26		2/10 EOM	?	?

31. Given the following, calculate cash discount and amount paid.

Gross amount of invoice including freight, $900
Freight, $100
Invoice date, 9/6
Terms, 1/10 EOM
Date of payment, 10/9

32. Calculate the amount to be credited and balance outstanding from the following partial payment information.

Invoice amount, $950
Terms, 2/10, n/60
Invoice date, 9/20
Partial payment date, 9/27
Partial payment, $400

33. A Goodyear Tire Shop received an invoice showing 5 tires at $40 each, 9 tires at $70 each and 20 tires at $90 each. Shipping terms are FOB shipping point. Freight is $200. Trade discount is 10/9 and a cash discount of 2/10, N/30 is offered. Assuming Goodyear pays within the discount period, what did Goodyear pay?

28. .19199
29. $216.20 net price;
$ 33.80 trade discount
30. **a.** July 18
Aug. 7
b. Apr. 10
Apr. 30
c. Oct. 14
Nov. 3
d. May 10
May 30
31. $8.00
$892
32. $408.16
$541.84
33. $2,310.89

Worked-Out Solutions to Calculations/Applications Section

27.
```
100%      100%      100%
- 15%     -  3%     -  2%
 .85  ×    .97  ×    .98   = .80801
```

28.
```
1.00000
- .80801
  .19199
```

29.
```
100%      100%                   1.0000
-  8%     -  6%                  - .8648
 .92  ×    .94   =    .8648 NPER    .1352 SEDR
                  ×  $250        ×  $250
                    $216.20         $33.80
```

30. **a.** July 8   189
```
        + 30
        219 → Aug. 7
```
c. Oct. 4   277
```
        + 30
        307 → Nov. 3
```

b. Cash discount ends after first 10 days of month that follows the sale. Credit period ends 20 days after discount period.

d. Cash discount ends after first 10 days of second month that follows the sale. Credit period ends 20 days after discount period.

31.
```
 $900
- 100
 $800 × .01 = $8.00
 $800 × .99 = $792 + $100 = $892
```

32. $\dfrac{\$400}{1 - .02} = \dfrac{\$400}{.98} = \$408.16$

```
  $950.00
- 408.16
  $541.84
```

33.
$$5 \times \$40 = \$\ 200$$
$$9 \times \$70 = \quad 630$$
$$20 \times \$90 = \underline{\quad 1,800}$$
$$\$2,630 \text{ total list}$$

100%	100%
− 10%	− 9%

$$.90 \ \times \ .91 \ = \qquad .819$$
$$\times \quad \underline{\$2,630}$$
$$\$2,153.97$$

$$\$2,153.97 \times .98 = \$2,110.89$$
$$+ \ \underline{200.00}$$
$$\$2,310.89$$

Word Problem Practice Quiz

Check with your instructor for complete worked-out solutions.

7–1. Alvin Corporation buys wood stoves from a wholesaler. The list price of a wood stove is $700, with a trade discount of 35%. Find the amount of trade discount and the net price of this stove.

7–2. Algene Bookstore paid a net price of $7,400 for the coming semester. The publisher offered a trade discount of 25%. What was the publisher's original list price?

7–3. Bob's Radio Shop wants to buy a line of new shortwave radios. Manufacturer A offers chain discounts of 19/10, while Manufacturer B offers terms of 18/11. Assume both manufacturers have the same list price. Which manufacturer should Bob buy from?

7–4. John's Dress Shop received an invoice dated November 8 for $1,619, with terms of 3/10, 2/15, n/60. On November 23, John's Dress Shop sent a partial payment of $715. What is the actual amount that should be credited? What is John's Dress Shop's outstanding balance?

7–5. An invoice dated 5/16/XX received by Jack's Supply indicated a balance of $7,200. This balance included a freight charge of $400. Terms of the bill were 3/10, 2/30, n/60. Assume Jack pays off the bill on May 25. What amount will he pay?

7–6. B Tool Manufacturer sold a set of jigsaws to Buy Hardware. The list price was $1,520. B Tool offered a chain discount of 4/3/2. What was the net price of the jigsaws, and what was the total of the trade discount? Round these two answers to nearest cent.

7–7. Smith of Boston sold office equipment for $12,500 to Frank of Los Angeles. Terms of the sale are 2/10, n/30 FOB Boston. Smith has agreed to prepay the freight of $120. Assume Frank pays within the discount period. How much will they pay Smith?

7–8. A manufacturer of ice skates offered chain discounts of 6/5/1 to many of its customers. Bob's Sporting Goods ordered 30 pairs of ice skates that had a total list price of $1,800. What was the net price paid by Bob's Sporting Goods? What was the amount of the trade discount? Round answers to nearest cent.

7–9. A living room set lists for $9,000 and carries a trade discount of 30%. Freight (FOB shipping point) of $70 is not part of list price. Calculate the net price (also include cost of freight) of the living room set assuming a cash discount of 4%. What was amount of trade discount?

7–10. An invoice dated February 9 in the amount of $45,000 is received by Reliance Corporation on February 13. Cash discount terms on the invoice are 2/10, n/30. On February 18, Reliance mails a check in the amount of $9,000 as partial payment on the invoice. What is the amount of discount Reliance should receive?

CHAPTER 8

Self-Paced Worksheet
(Items with an asterisk (*) are not covered in the Brief Edition.)

Cover the answers on the right and fill in each blank. After answering the question, look to the right for your answer.

Vocabulary Review

1. The _____ _____ is the selling price less cost.
2. Gross profit minus operating expenses equals net _____.
3. The _____ is the price paid to supplier to bring merchandise into the store.
4. The original selling price less the reduction to sale price equals the _____ _____.
5. Net sales minus costs equals _____ _____.
6. Cost plus markup equals _____ _____.
7. The regular expenses of doing business are called _____ expenses.
8. Dollar markup divided by cost equals _____ _____ on _____.
9. Dollar markup divided by selling price equals _____ _____ on _____ _____.
10. The dollar markdown divided by the original selling price equals _____ _____.

1.	dollar markup
2.	income
3.	cost
4.	dollar markdown
5.	gross profit
6.	selling price
7.	operating
8.	percent markup; cost
9.	percent markup; selling price
10.	markdown percent

Theory Tips (and/or Cautions)

11. When markup is based on cost the cost is assumed to be _____ percent.
12. Selling price equals _____ plus markup.
13. The dollar markup divided by percent markup on cost equals the _____.
14. When markup is based on cost, the cost is the _____.
15. When markup is based on cost, the portion is the _____ _____.
16. When markup is based on selling price, the selling price is assumed to be _____ percent.
17. The dollar markup divided by percent markup on selling price equals the _____ _____.
18. When markup is based on selling price, the selling price is the _____.
19. When markup is based on selling price, the portion is the _____.
20. In markdowns, the dollar markdown is the _____.
21. The _____ _____ _____ in a markdown is considered to be the base.
22.* For perishables, markup is based on _____.

11.	100
12.	cost
13.	cost
14.	base
15.	selling price
16.	100
17.	selling price
18.	base
19.	cost
20.	portion
21.	original selling price
22.	cost

Calculations/Applications

Do calculations on scrap paper as needed. Worked-out solutions are provided at end.

23. Neal Wall bought a computer from A.C. Suppliers for $1,200. Neal plans to resell the computer for $1,800. What is Neal Wall's dollar markup and his percent markup on cost? Check your answer.
24. Fred Miguel bought rings for his jewelry shop that cost $90 each. Fred must mark up each ring 40% on cost. What is the dollar markup? What is the selling price of each ring? Check your answer.
25. Alice Rone sells watches. Her competitor sells a new line of watches for $30 each. Alice needs a 30% markup on cost to make her desired profit, and she must meet price competition. What cost can Alice afford to bring these watches into the store? What is the dollar markup?

23.	$600 markup; 50% markup on cost
24.	$36; $126
25.	$23.08; $6.92

26. Neal Wall bought a computer from A.C. Suppliers for $1,200. Neal plans to resell the computer for $1,800. What is Neal Wall's dollar markup and his percent markup on selling price? (Round to the nearest tenth percent.)

27. Fred Miguel bought rings for his jewelry shop that cost $90 each. Fred must mark up each ring 40% on selling price. What is the selling price of each ring? What is the dollar markup? Check your answer.

28. Alice Rone sells watches. Her competitor sells a new line of watches for $30 each. Alice needs a 30% markup on selling price to make her desired profit, and she must meet price competition. What cost can Alice afford to bring these watches into the store? What is the dollar markup?

29. Pete Burrows sells hammers for $14 that cost $8. What is Pete's percent markup at cost? (Round to the nearest tenth percent.) What is Pete's percent markup on selling price? (Round to the nearest hundredth percent.)

30. Staples bought an office desk for $400 and marked it up 30% on selling price to promote customer interest. Staples marked the desk down 5% for one week. After a week, Staples marked the desk up 2%. The last week it marked it down 8%. What is the final selling price?

31.* Joe Kiim owns a bakery. Joe baked 40 dozen bagels. Joe expects a 20% spoilage rate. The bagels cost $1.10 per dozen. Joe wants a 70% markup on cost. What should Joe charge for each dozen bagels? (Round to the nearest cent.)

Worked-Out Solutions to Calculations/Applications Section

23. $1,800 - $1,200 = $600 $\qquad$ $\dfrac{$600}{$1,200} = 50\%$

   Check: $\dfrac{$600}{.50} = $1,200$

24. $S = C + M$
   $S = $90 + .40($90)$
   $S = $90 + 36 $\qquad$ or $\qquad$ Check: $1.40 \times $90 = 126
   $S = 126

25.* $\quad S = C + M$
   $$30 = C + .30C$
   $\dfrac{$30}{1.30} = \dfrac{1.30C}{1.30}$ $\qquad$ or $\qquad$ $\dfrac{$30}{1 + .30} = \dfrac{$30}{1.30} = 23.08
   $$23.08 = C$
   $$30 - $23.08 = 6.92 markup

26. $\quad S = C + M$
   $$1,800 = $1,200 + M$
   $$600 = M$
   $\dfrac{$600}{$1,800} = 33.3\%$

27.* $\quad S = C + M$
   $\quad S = $90 + .40S$
   $-.40S \qquad\qquad -.40S$
   $\dfrac{.60S}{.60} = \dfrac{$90}{.60}$ $\qquad$ or $\qquad$ $\dfrac{$90}{1 - .40} = \dfrac{$90}{.60} = 150
   $\quad S = 150
   $$150 - $90 = 60 markup

28.* $\quad S = C + M$
   $$30 = C + .30 ($30)$
   $$30 = C + 9 $\qquad$ or $\qquad$ $C = $30(1 - .30)$
   $-9 \qquad\qquad -9 \qquad\qquad\quad C = $30(.70)$
   $\overline{$21 = C} \qquad\qquad\qquad\quad C = 21
   $$30 - $21 = 9 markup

29. $14
   $\dfrac{-\ 8}{$\ 6}$ $\quad \dfrac{$6}{$8} = 75\%$ $\quad \dfrac{$6}{$14} = 42.86\%$

30.*

$$S = C + M$$
$$S = \$400 + .30S$$

$$\begin{array}{ccc} -.30S & -.30S \\ \hline \dfrac{.70S}{.70} = \dfrac{\$400}{.70} & \end{array} \quad \text{or} \quad \dfrac{\$400}{1-.30} = \dfrac{\$400}{.70} = \$571.43$$

$$S = \$571.43$$

$\$571.43 \times .95 = \$542.86$
$\$542.86 \times 1.02 = \$553.71$
$\$553.71 \times .92 = \$509.41$

31. $TS = TC + TM$

$TS = \$44 + .70(\$44)$ $\$1.10 \times 40 = \$44 \; TC$

$TS = \$74.80$

$\dfrac{\$74.80}{32} = \$2.34$ per dozen

Word Problem Practice Quiz

Check with your instructor for complete worked-out solutions.

8–1. A computer sells for $820 and is marked up 40% of the selling price. What is the cost of the computer?

8–2. Bob Hoffman sells a radio for $189.19 that cost him $91.50. What was Bob's percent of markup based on the selling price? Round to nearest percent. Check your answer. Will be slightly off due to rounding.

8–3. Reese Company buys a watch at a cost of $48.50. Reese plans to sell the watch for $79.99. What is the dollar markup as well as percent markup on cost? Round to nearest hundredth percent. Check your answer. Will be slightly off due to rounding.

8–4. Bill Spread, owner of the Bedding Shop, knows that his customers will pay no more than $300 for a comforter. Assume Bill wants a 30% markup on selling price. What is the most he could pay the manufacturer for this comforter?

8–5. John Mills sells ski gloves. He knows the most that people will pay for the gloves is $39.99. John is convinced that he needs a 28% markup based on cost. What is the most that John can pay to his supplier for gloves and still keep his selling price constant? Round to nearest cent.

8–6 Al's Department Store bought a sterling silver set for $518. Jim wants to mark up the set at 48% of the selling price. What should be the selling price of the sterling set? Round to nearest cent.

8–7. At the end of the summer, lawn mowers were advertised for 35% off regular price. John Mills saw a lawn mower with a regular price of $199. What is the dollar markdown as well as the sale price?

8–8. Mr. Fry, store manager for Vic's Appliance, is having a difficult time placing a selling price on a refrigerator that cost $899. Mr. Fry knows his boss would like to have a 35% markup based on cost. Could you help Mr. Fry with the calculation?

8–9. Angie's Bake Shop makes decorated chocolate chip cookies that cost $.30 each. Past experience shows that 20% of the cookies will crack and have to be discarded. Assume Angie wants a 65% markup based on cost and produces 400 cookies. What price should each cookie sell for? Round to nearest cent.

8–10. If, in Problem 8–9, the cracked cookies could be sold for $.20 each, what should the selling price per cookie be?

CHAPTER 9

Self-Paced Worksheet

Cover the answers on the right and fill in each blank. After answering the question, look to the right for your answer.

Vocabulary Review

1. _____ means being paid 26 times in a year.
2. The ____ ____ ____ ____ sets minimum wage standards and overtime regulations.
3. _____ _____ represents earnings before deductions.
4. A _____ _____ schedule is based on different levels of production.
5. A _____ represents an advance that will have to be repaid.
6. A _____ _____ scale uses different commission rates for different levels of net sales.
7. FICA tax requires separate reporting for _____ _____ and _____.
8. The _____ _____ method or the _____ method may be used to calculate amount of federal income tax withheld.
9. _____ _____ _____ may vary from state to state.
10. A _____ _____ is a multicolumn form to record payroll.

Theory Tips (and/or Cautions)

11. A _____ is made up of thirteen weeks.
12. Biweekly period is 26 times per year, while _____ is 24 times.
13. If an overtime rate is grater than two decimal places _____ _____ round it.
14. Net pay plus _____ equals gross pay.
15. A draw is an _____ on a salesperson's commission.
16. The taxable earnings column of a _____ _____ shows the wages subject to the tax, not the actual deduction.
17. _____ has no base cut off while Social Security does.
18. The _____ _____ is used by companies that do not want to store wage bracket tables.
19. The _____ pays for state and federal unemployment.

Calculations/Applications

Do calculations on scrap paper as needed. Worked-out solutions are provided at end.

20. Calculate the total gross pay for Melvin Moore. Assume time and half for overtime. Melvin earns $8 per hour.

    Melvin's hours worked

M	T	W	Th	F	Sat
5	12	8	7	9	14

21. Based on the following schedule, what is Ron's gross pay? Ron had net sales of $180,000.

Up to $40,000	6%
$40,000–$60,000	7%
Over $60,000	$7\frac{1}{2}$%

22. Assume a 6.20% Social Security rate on $61,200 and a Medicare rate of 1.45%. What will Alice pay in, for Social Security and Medicare for this week's payroll of $1,500? To date, her cumulative earnings before this payroll were $60,000.

1.	biweekly
2.	Fair Labor Standards Act
3.	gross pay
4.	differential pay
5.	draw
6.	variable commission
7.	Social Security; Medicare
8.	wage bracket; percentage
9.	State unemployment tax
10.	payroll register
11.	quarter
12.	semimonthly
13	do not
14.	deductions
15.	advance
16.	payroll register
17.	Medicare
18.	percentage method
19.	employer
20.	$500
21.	$12,800
22.	SS $74.40; Med $21.75

23. From the following information, calculate Pat's net pay. Use the wage bracket table for FIT.

Employee	Status	Claims	Gross pay	FIT	FICA SS/Med	Net pay
Pat Swan	M	2	$930			

24. Redo #23 using the percentage method in calculating FIT.

25. Lloyd Alex has two employees who earn $500 and $800 a week. Assume a 5.4% FUTA rate. What will Lloyd pay for SUTA and FUTA for the first quarter?

Worked-Out Solutions to Calculations/Applications Section

20. Total hours   = 55
40 hours × $8   = $320
15 hours × $12 = 180
                $500

21. ($40,000 × .06) + ($20,000 × .07) + ($120,000 × .075)
     $2,400 + $1,400 + $9,000 = $12,800

22. **Social Security**   **Medicare**

  $61,200 $1,500 × .0145 = $21.75
 − 60,000

  $ 1,200 × .062 = $74.40

23. FIT: $109 by table
SS: $930 × .062   = $57.66
Med: $930 × .0145 = $13.49
Net pay: $930 − $109 − $57.66 − $13.49 = $749.85

24. FIT $930.00
        − 96.16 ($48.08 × 2)
        $833.84

FIT   = $105.75 + .28($5.84) ← $833.84 − $828
       = $105.75 + $1.64 = $107.39

Net pay = $930 − $107.39 − $57.66 − $13.49 = $751.46

25.   Exempt wages
13 weeks × $500 = $ 6,500   –0–
13 weeks × $800 = $10,400 $3,400
             $16,900

$16,900 − $3,400 = $13,500 taxable wages

SUTA: .054 × $13,500 = $729
FUTA: .008 × $13,500 = $108

Word Problem Practice Quiz

Check with your instructor for complete worked-out solutions.

9–1. Read Jones is a salesclerk at Moe's Department Store. She is paid $7.50 per hour plus a commission of 3% on all sales. Assume Read works 35 hours and has sales of $4,800. What is her gross pay?

9–2. Staple Corporation pays its employees on a graduated commission scale: 5% on the first $40,000 sales; 6% on sales above $40,000 to $85,000; and 7% on sales greater than $85,000. Bill Burns had sales of $92,000. What commission did Bill earn?

9–3. John Hall earned $1,060 last week. He is married, paid biweekly, and claims two exemptions, What is his income tax? Use the percentage method.

9–4. Larry Johnson earns a gross salary of $3,000 each week. In week 25 what will Larry pay for Social Security and Medicare taxes?

9–5. Robyn Hartman earns $700 per week plus 5% of sales in excess of $7,000. If Robyn sells $20,000 the first week, how much are her earnings?

9–6. Joe Ross is an automobile salesman who receives a salary of $400 per week plus a commission of 6% on all sales. During a 4-week period he sold $46,900 worth of cars. What were Joe's average earnings?

9–7. B. Smith is a manager for Alve Corp. His earnings are subject to deductions for Social Security, Medicare, and FIT. B. Smith is $950 below the maximum for Social Security. What will his net pay for the week be if he earns $1,200? B. Smith is married, paid weekly, and claims three exemptions. Assume Social Security rate is 6.2% on $61,200 and Medicare is 1.45%. Use the wage bracket table for FIT.

9–8. Al Write is a salesman who receives a $1,600 draw per week. He receives a 12% commission on all sales. Sales for Al were $192,000 for the month. What did Al receive after taking the draw into consideration? Assume a 5-week month.

9–9. Angel Frank has a cumulative earnings of $61,100 at the end of June. The first week in July she earns $1,100. What is the total amount deducted for Social Security and Medicare?

9–10. Pete Lowe, who is single and paid monthly, earns $3,300 per month. He claims a withholding allowance of one. How much FIT is deducted from his paycheck using the percentage method?

CHAPTER 10

Self-Paced Worksheet

Cover the answers on the right and fill in each blank. After answering the question, look to the right for your answer.

Vocabulary Review

1. The annual _____ _____ forces savings institutions to reveal their real or true rate of interest.

2. The exact time, ordinary interest method is known as the _____ _____.

3. _____ _____ equals principal plus interest.

4. _____ _____ represents the cost of a loan.

5. The _____ _____, exact interest method is used by the Federal Reserve banks and the federal government.

6. _____ interest uses 360 days.

7. The _____ is the amount of money that is originally borrowed, loaned, or deposited.

8. The U.S. _____ allows the borrower to receive proper interest credits when paying off a loan in more than one payment before the maturity date.

9. The _____ _____ _____ is principal times rate times time.

10. _____ can be expressed as years or fractional years, used to calculate the simple interest.

1.	percentage yield
2.	Banker's Rule
3.	maturity value
4.	simple interest
5.	exact time
6.	ordinary
7.	principal
8.	Rule
9.	simple interest formula
10.	time

Theory Tips (and/or Cautions)

11. _____ time periods can be days, months, or years.

12. Exact time can be found by the table in the *Business Math Handbook*, while _____ _____ represents 365 days.

13. The exact time, ordinary interest results in _____ interest than the exact time exact interest method.

14. In calculating the time in a cash discount versus borrowing problem, the time would be the _____ between the credit and discount period.

15. In solving for the principal, given the interest, rate, and time the denominator will _____ _____ rounded.

16. When finding the time it can be converted to _____ by multiplying it by 360 or 365.

17. In the U.S. Rule, any partial payment is applied to cover the _____ due before the remainder of payment is used to lower the principal.

18. The last step of the U.S. Rule at maturity is to calculate interest from the last partial payment and _____ this interest to the adjusted balance.

19. In the U.S. Rule, the numerator of the interest calculation represents the _____ _____ _____ from previous payment date and goes to new payment date.

11.	loan
12.	exact interest
13.	higher
14.	difference
15.	not be
16.	days
17.	interest
18.	add
19.	number of days

Calculations/Applications

Do calculations on scrap paper as needed. Worked-out solutions are provided at end.

20. Simple interest on $15,000 at $4\frac{1}{2}$% for 8 months is _____.

21. Simple interest on $20,000 at $7\frac{1}{2}$% for 17 months is _____.

22. On June 8, Reed Ching borrowed $18,000 at 7%. Reed must pay the principal and interest on September 4. Using the exact time, exact interest method, the maturity value is _____.

23. The maturity value in #22 would be _____ using the exact time, ordinary interest method.

24. Fred Sullivan bought a new CD-ROM computer for $2,500 with 2/10, n/30 terms. Assume Fred pays for the computer with 11% borrowed funds to take advantage of the cash discount. His net savings would be _____ using exact time, ordinary interest.

20.	$450
21.	$2,125
22.	$18,303.78
23.	$18,308
24.	$35.03

25. Complete the following (assume 360 days).

	Principal	Rate	Time	Simple interest
a.	?	6%	90 days	$18,000
b.	$6,000	?	300 days	$400
c.	$2,500	$7\frac{1}{2}$%	?	$550

26. Aray Foger borrowed $7,000 for 60 days at 7%. On day 20, Aray made a $800 partial payment. On day 45, Aray made a $1,200 partial payment. What is Aray's ending balance under the U.S. Rule?

Worked-Out Solutions to Calculations/Applications Section

20. $15,000 \times .045 \times \frac{8}{12} = $450

21. $20,000 \times .075 \times \frac{17}{12} = $2,125

22. Sept 4 → 247
June 8 → $\frac{159}{88}$

$$\$18,000 \times .07 \times \frac{88}{365} = \$303.78$$

$$MV = \$18,000 + \$303.78 = \$18,303.78$$

23. $$\$18,000 \times .07 \times \frac{88}{360} = \$308$$

$$MV = \$18,000 + \$308 = \$18,308$$

24. $2,500 \times .02 = $50

$$\$2,450 \times .11 \times \frac{20}{360} = \$14.97$$

Savings: $50 − $14.97 = $35.03

25. **a.** $$\frac{\$18,000}{.06 \times \frac{90}{360}} = \$1,200,000$$

b. $$\frac{\$400}{\$6,000 \times \frac{300}{360}} = .08 = 8\%$$

c. $$\frac{\$550}{\$2,500 \times .075} = 2.9\overline{3} \times 360 = 1,056 \text{ days}$$

26. $$\$7,000 \times .07 \times \frac{20}{360} = \$27.22$$

$$
\begin{array}{r}
\$800.00 \\
- \ 27.22 \\
\hline
\$772.78
\end{array}
$$

$$
\begin{array}{r}
\$7,000.00 \\
- \ 772.78 \\
\hline
\end{array}
$$

$$\$6,227.22 \times .07 \times \frac{25}{360} = \$30.27$$

$$
\begin{array}{r}
\$1,200.00 \\
- \ 30.27 \\
\hline
\$1,169.73
\end{array}
$$

$$
\begin{array}{r}
\$6,227.22 \\
-1,169.73 \\
\hline
\end{array}
$$

$$\$5,057.49 \times .07 \times \frac{15}{360} = \$14.75$$

Balance owed $5,072.24 ($14.75 + $5,057.49)

Word Problem Practice Quiz

Check with your instructor for complete worked-out solutions.

10–1. Abby Ellen took out a loan of $45,000 to pay for her child's education. The loan would be repaid at the end of 8 years in one payment with $12\frac{1}{2}$% interest. How much interest is due? What is the total amount Abby has to pay at the end of the loan?

10–2. Bill Blane bought a computer printer for $500 with terms of 2/10, n/60. The truth is that Bill doesn't have the cash to take advantage of the cash discount. His aunt told him to borrow the money from Roe Bank at the current rate of 11% and take advantage of the cash discount. Bill feels the cash discount doesn't warrant taking out a loan. Present your case to Bill (use 360 days in a year).

10–3. Jennifer Rick went to Sunshine Bank to borrow $3,500 at a rate of $10\frac{3}{4}$%. The date of the loan was September 7. Jennifer hoped to repay the loan on January 15. Assume the loan is on exact time, ordinary interest. What will be the interest cost on January 15? How much will Jennifer totally repay?

10–4. Jill Blum has a talk with Jennifer Rick (Problem 10–3) and suggests she consider the loan on exact time, exact interest. Recalculate the loan for Jennifer under this assumption.

10–5. Bob Lopes visited his local bank to see how long it will take for $1,000 to amount to $1,900 at a simple interest rate of 10%. Can you solve Bob's problem?

10–6. Margie Jones owns her own car. Her November monthly interest was $205. The rate is $13\frac{1}{2}$%. Find out what Margie's principal balance is at the beginning of November. Use 360 days. (In calculation, do not round denominator answer before dividing into numerator.)

10–7. Jane took out a loan for $16,800 at $9\frac{3}{4}$% on April 2, 1996. The loan is due January 8, 1997. Using exact time, ordinary interest, what is the interest cost? What total amount will Jane pay on January 8, 1997?

10–8. Terry Ball took out the same loan as Jane (Problem 10–7), but his terms were exact time, exact interest. What is Terry's difference in interest? What will Terry pay on January 8, 1997?

10–9. Bill Brody borrowed $12,500 on an 11% 120-day note. After 65 days, Bill paid $500 toward the note. On day 89, Bill paid an additional $4,500. What is the final balance due? Work out the total interest and ending balance due by the U.S. Rule.

CHAPTER 11

Self-Paced Worksheet

Cover the answers on the right and fill in each blank. After answering the question, look to the right for your answer.

Vocabulary Review

1. For a simple discount note the interest banks deduct in advance is the _____ _____.
2. Principal plus interest equals _____ _____.
3. The _____ _____ is also the principal of the note.
4. The company extending credit of an interest-bearing note is called the _____.
5. The company issuing the note and borrowing the money is called the _____.
6. A _____ note states that the borrower will repay a certain sum at a fixed time in the future.
7. The _____ of the note represents what one receives after deducting the bank discount from the maturity value of a note.
8. The _____ _____ is the true rate of interest.
9. A _____ _____ represents a loan to the federal government.
10. A _____ _____ _____ provides immediate financing up to an approved limit.

1. bank discount
2. maturity value
3. face value
4. payee
5. maker
6. promissory
7. proceeds
8. effective rate
9. Treasury bill
10. line of credit

Theory Tips (and/or Cautions)

11. The _____ _____ of the a non-interest-bearing note is the same as its face value.
12. A promissory note for a loan is usually _____ than one year.
13. The _____ _____ is higher for a simple discount note, since interest is deducted in advance.
14. The purchase price (or proceeds) of a Treasury bill is the value of the Treasury bill _____ the discount.
15. In the discounting process, the discount period represents the number of days the _____ will have to wait for the note to come due.
16. Instead of discounting notes, many companies set up _____ _____ _____ so that additional financing is immediately available.
17. A _____ _____ can be interest-bearing or noninterest-bearing.
18. In discounting an interest-bearing note before maturity, the first step is to calculate the _____ _____.
19. To calculate the _____ _____ you must use the maturity value times the bank discount rate times the number of days the bank waits for the note to come due divided by 360.

11. maturity value
12. less
13. effective rate
14. less
15. bank
16. lines of credit
17. promissory note
18. maturity value
19. bank discount

Calculations/Applications

Do calculations on scrap paper as needed. Worked-out solutions are provided at end.

20. Andre Fox borrowed $15,000 on a noninterest-bearing, simple discount, $7\frac{1}{2}$%, 90-day note. Assume exact time, ordinary interest. What is (a) maturity value, (b) the bank's discount, (c) Andre's proceeds, and (d) the effective rate to nearest hundredth percent?

21. Joy Lindman buys a $10,000 13-week Treasury bill at $8\frac{1}{4}$%. What is her effective rate? Round to the nearest hundredth percent.

22. Frost Corporation accepted a $20,000, 8%, 90-day note on July 8. Frost discounts the note on September 6 at East Bank at 9%. What proceeds did Frost receive?

20. **a.** $15,000;
    b. $281.25;
    c. $14,718.75;
    d. 7.64%;
21. 8.42%
22. $20,247

Worked-Out Solutions to Calculations/Applications Section

20. b. $\$15,000 \times .075 \times \dfrac{90}{360} = \$281.25$

c. $\$15,000 - \$281.25 = \$14,718.75$

d. $\dfrac{\$281.25}{\$14,718.75 \times \dfrac{90}{360}} = 7.64\%$

21. $\$10,000 \times .0825 \times \dfrac{13}{52} = \$206.25$

$\$10,000 - \$206.25 = \$9,793.75$

$\dfrac{\$206.25}{\$9,793.75 \times \dfrac{13}{52}} = 8.42\%$

22. Interest $= \$20,000 \times .08 \times \dfrac{90}{360} = \$400$

1. $MV = \$20,000 + \$400 = \$20,400$

2. Sept. 6 → 249
   July 8 → $\underline{189}$
   $\qquad\qquad 60 \qquad 90 - 60 = 30$ days

3. Bank discount $= \$20,400 \times .09 \times \dfrac{30}{360} = \$153$

4. Proceeds $= \$20,400 - \$153 = \$20,247$

Word Problem Practice Quiz

Check with your instructor for complete worked-out solutions.

Use ordinary interest in your calculations.

11–1. James Bank discounts an 89-day note for $15,000 at 12%. Find the bank discount and proceeds.

11–2. In Problem 11–1, what is the effective rate of interest when the bank discounts the note at 12%? Round to nearest hundredth percent.

11–3. Jarvis Corporation accepted an $18,000 note on August 12. Terms of the note were $12\frac{3}{4}\%$ for 90 days. Jarvis discounted the note on September 20 at Shaw Bank at 13%. What net proceeds did Jarvis receive?

11–4. Michele Fross borrowed $6,000 for 120 days from Jones Bank. The bank discounted the note at 9%. What proceeds does Michele receive? Calculate effective interest rate to nearest hundredth percent.

11–5. On November 30, Smith Company accepted a 120-day, $15,000 noninterest-bearing note from B Manufacturer. What is the maturity value of the note?

11–6. On July 12 at the Sunshine Bank, Joyce Corporation discounted a $5,000, 90-day note dated June 20. Sunshine's discount rate was $11\frac{3}{4}\%$. How much did Joyce Corporation receive? Assume $5,000 is the maturity value.

11–7. Roger Corporation accepted an $8,000, 11%, 120-day note dated August 8 from June Company in settlement of a past bill. On October 25, Roger Corporation discounted the note at the bank at 12%. What is the note's maturity value, discount period, and bank discount? What are the net proceeds to Roger Corporation?

11–8. On April 12, Dr. Brown accepted a $10,000, 10%, 60-day note from Bill Moss granting a time extension on a past-due account. Dr. Brown discounted the note at the bank at 12% on May 20. What proceeds does Dr. Brown receive?

11–9. On May 5, Scott Rinse accepted a $12,000 note in granting a time extension of a bill for goods bought by Ron Prentice. Terms of the note were 13% for 90 days. On July 2, Scott could no longer wait for the money and discounted the note at Able Bank at 11%. What are Scott's proceeds?

11–10. Jensen Furniture wants to buy a $5,000 computer with a huge $1,000 cash discount. Jensen needs more cash to pay the bill. It is considering discounting a 120-day note dated May 12 with a maturity value of $5,000. Hunt Bank has a discount rate of 15% on May 18. Should Jensen discount the note?

CHAPTER 12

Self-Paced Worksheet

Cover the answers on the right and fill in each blank. After answering the question, look to the right for your answer.

Vocabulary Review

1. _____ is calculating the interest periodically over the life of the loan and adding it to the principal.
2. _____ _____ looks at how much money will have to be deposited today (or at some date) to reach a specific amount at maturity (in the future).
3. _____ are calculated by the number of years times the number of times compounded per year.
4. The _____ can be found by the annual rate divided by the number of times compounded per year.
5. Compounded _____ means the interest is calculated on the balance every six months.
6. The _____ _____ is calculated by the interest for 1 year divided by the principal.
7. The stated or _____ rate is one which the bank calculates interest.

1. compounding
2. present value
3. periods
4. rate
5. semiannually
6. effective rate
7. nominal

Theory Tips (and/or Cautions)

8. To see how long to double a sum of money at different interest rates with annual compounding, divide 72 by the _____ _____.
9. Compounding goes from the present value to the _____ _____.
10. Present value goes from the future value to the _____ _____.
11. Compounded _____ means interest is calculated on the balance every 3 months.
12. Compound amounts less the principal equals _____ _____.
13. Compounding results in _____ interest than simple interest.
14. In the calculation of effective rate, the portion is the _____ for one year.
15. Effective rate for $1 can be seen in the _____ table.
16. The table factors in the _____ _____ table are larger than 1.
17. The table factors in the _____ _____ table are less than 1.
18;. A present value answer can be checked by using the _____ _____ table.

8. interest rate
9. future value
10. present value
11. quarterly
12. compound interest
13. higher
14. interest
15. compound
16. compound interest
17. present value
18. compound value

Calculations/Applications

Do calculations on scrap paper as needed. Worked-out solutions are provided at end.

19. Alfred Rodriguez deposits $8,000 in Yoma Bank which pays 6% interest compounded quarterly. How much will Alfred have in his account at the end of 6 years?
20. Give the following, calculate the effective rate (to the nearest hundredth percent): Principal, $9,000; Interest rate, 8% compounded semiannually.
21. $1,800 compounded daily for 10 years will grow to _____ at 6.50%.
22. Jim Henson wants to buy his son a Toyota Land Cruiser in 5 years. The cost of the car should be $40,000. Assuming a bank rate of 6% compounded quarterly, how much must Jim put in the bank today?
23. Check your answer in #22 by the compound table.

19. $11,436
20. 8.16%
21. $3,447.72
22. $29,700
23. $40,002

Worked-Out Solutions to Calculations/Applications Section

19. $\frac{6\%}{4} = 1.5\%$ 6 yrs. $\times$ 4 = 24 periods

    $8,000 $\times$ 1.4295 = $11,436

20. 4%, 2 periods (2 $\times$ 1)

    $9,000 $\times$ 1.0816 = $9,734.40
     − 9,000.00
     $\overline{\$\ 734.40}$

    $\frac{\$734.40}{\$9,000} = 8.16\%$

21. $1,800 \times 1.9154 = \$3,447.72$

22. $\dfrac{6\%}{4} = 1\frac{1}{2}\%$ 5 yrs. $\times$ 4 = 20 periods

$40,000 \times .7425 = \$29,700$

23. $1\frac{1}{2}\%$, 20 periods   1.3469

$29,700 \times 1.3469 = \$40,002$ off slightly due to rounding of table factors.

Word Problem Practice Quiz

Check with your instructor for complete worked-out solutions.

12–1. Al Baker deposited $30,000 into Victory Bank which pays 12% interest compounded semiannually. How much will Al have in his account at the end of 4 years?

12–2. Ann Kate, owner of Ann's Sport Shop, loaned $13,000 to Rusty Katz to help him open an art shop. Rusty pans to repay Ann at the end of 5 years with 6% interest compounded quarterly. How much will Ann receive at the end of 5 years?

12–3. Jill Fonda opened a new savings account. She deposited $18,000 at 12% interest compounded semiannually. At the beginning of the year 4, Jill deposits an additional $50,000 that is also compounded semiannually at 12%. At the end of 6 years, what is the balance in Jill's account?

12–4. Rochelle Kotter wants to attend S.M.V. University. She will need $55,000 4 years from today. Her bank pays 12% interest compounded semiannually. What amount must Rochelle deposit today so she will have $55,000 in 4 years?

12–5. Margaret Foster wants to buy a new camper in 7 years. Margaret estimates the cost of the camper will be $7,200. If she invests $4,000 now, at a rate of 12% interest compounded semiannually, will she have enough money to buy her camper at the end of 7 years?

12–6. Karen is having difficulty deciding whether to put her savings in Mystic Bank or in Four Rivers Bank. Mystic offers a 10% interest rate compounded semiannually, while Four Rivers offers 12% interest compounded annually. Karen has $30,000 to deposit and expects to withdraw the money at the end of 5 years. Which bank gives Karen the best deal?

12–7. Steven deposited $15,000 at York Bank at 10% interest compounded semiannually. What was the effective rate? Round to nearest hundredth percent.

12–8. Al Miller, owner of Al's Garage, estimates that he will need $25,000 for new equipment in 20 years. Al decided to put aside the money today so it will be available in 20 years. His bank offers him 8% interest compounded semiannually. How much must Al invest today to have $25,000 in 20 years?

12–9. Ray Long wants to retire in Arizona when he is 70 years of age. He is now 55 and believes he will need $200,000 to retire comfortably. To date, Ray has set aside no retirement money. Assume Ray gets 12% interest compounded semiannually. How much must be invest today to meet his goal of $200,000?

12–10. Kevin Moore deposited $12,000 in a new savings account at 6% interest compounded quarterly. At the beginning of year 4, Kevin deposits an additional $40,000 also compounded quarterly at 6%. At the end of 6 years, what is the balance in Kevin's account?

CHAPTER 13

Self-Paced Worksheet

Cover the answers on the right and fill in each blank. After answering the question, look to the right for the answer.

Vocabulary Review

1. An _____ is a stream of equal payments made at periodic times.
2. An _____ _____ is an annuity that is paid (or received) at the end of the time period.
3. An _____ _____ is an annuity that is paid (or received) at the beginning of the time period.
4. Annuities that have stated beginning and ending dates are called _____ _____.
5. Beginning and ending dates of _____ _____ are uncertain (not fixed).
6. A _____ _____ is an annuity in which the stream of deposits with appropriate interest will equal a specified amount in the future.
7. The _____ _____ _____ _____ is the amount of money needed today to receive a specified steam (annuity) of money in the future.

Theory Tips (and/or Cautions)

8. The value of an annuity is the value of a series of payments _____ interest.
9. With an ordinary annuity, regular payments (or deposits) are made at the _____ of the period.
10. With an annuity due, regular payments (or deposits) are made at the _____ of the period.
11. What we call _____ _____ in compounding is now called the value of annuity.
12. Ordinary annuities and annuities due both find _____ _____.
13. The _____ _____ will give a higher final value than _____ _____ since money is put in at the beginning of the period.
14. The _____ _____ of an ordinary annuity finds the present worth.
15. In calculating annuity due by the ordinary annuity table, you should add _____ period and subtract _____ payment.
16. Annuity payments do not have to be _____.
17. The sinking fund payment can be checked by the _____ _____ table.
18. In a sinking fund you determine the amount of _____ _____ you need to achieve a financial goal.

Calculations/Applications

Do calculations on scrap paper as needed. Worked-out solutions are provided at end.

19. Calculate by table the value of an investment after 3 years on an ordinary annuity of $6,000 made semiannually at 6%.
20. Redo your calculation in #19 assuming an annuity due.
21. Nancy Cram won the Boston Lottery and will receive a $5,000 check at the beginning of each 6 months for the next 7 years. If Nancy deposits each check into an account that pays 8%, how much will she have at the end of the 7 years?
22. What must you invest today to receive a $6,000 annuity for 10 years quarterly at 8% annual rate? All withdrawals will be made at the end of each period.
23. Pete O'Sullivan wants to set up a scholarship fund to provide 6 $4,000 scholarships for the next 5 years. If money can be invested at an annual rate of 6%, how much should Pete invest today?

Answers:

1. annuity
2. ordinary annuity
3. annuity due
4. annuities certain
5. contingent annuities
6. sinking fund
7. present value of annuity
8. plus
9. end
10. beginning
11. maturity value
12. future value
13. annuity due; ordinary annuity
14. present value
15. one; one
16. yearly
17. ordinary annuity
18. periodic payment
19. $38,810.40
20. $39,975
21. $95,118
22. $164,132.40
23. $101,097.60

24. Long Co. issued bonds that will mature to a value of $80,000 in 8 years. Long is setting up a sinking fund. Interest rates are 8% compounded quarterly. What will be the amount of each sinking fund payment? Verify your answer by the amount of annuity. It will be off due to rounding of tables. (Use tables in *Business Math Handbook*.)

Worked-Out Solutions to Calculations/Applications Section

19. $\frac{6\%}{2} = 3\%$ 3 yrs. $\times$ 2 = 6 periods

$6,000 $\times$ 6.4684 = $38,810.40

20. 3%, 7 periods

$6,000 $\times$ 7.6625 = $45,975
$- 6,000$
$\overline{\$39,975}$

21. $\frac{8\%}{2} = 4\%$ 7 yrs. $\times$ 2 = 14
$\phantom{\frac{8\%}{2} = 4\%   7 yrs. \times 2 =}\underline{+1}$
$\phantom{\frac{8\%}{2} = 4\%   7 yrs. \times 2 =}$15 periods

$5,000 $\times$ 20.0236 = $100,118
$\underline{-5,000}$
$\$95,118$

22. $\frac{8\%}{4} = 2\%$ 10 yrs. $\times$ 4 = 40 periods

$6,000 $\times$ 27.3554 = $164,132.40

23. 6%, 5 periods
$24,000 $\times$ 4.2124 = $101,097.60

24. $\frac{8\%}{4} = 2\%$ 8 yrs. $\times$ 4 = 32 periods

$80,000 $\times$ .0226 = $1,808
Verify: $1,808 $\times$ 44.2269 = $79,962 (due to rounding of tables)

Word Problem Practice Quiz

Check with your instructor for complete worked-out solutions.

13–1. Charlie Gold made deposits of $700 at end of each year for 7 years. The interest rate is 7% compounded annually. What is the value of Charlie's annuity at end of 7 years?

13–2. James Will promised to pay his son $500 semiannually for 5 years. Assume James can invest his money at 8% in an ordinary annuity. How much must James invest today to pay his son $500 semiannually for 5 years?

13–3. Bill Martin invests $6,000 at the end of each year for 7 years in an ordinary annuity at 6% interest compounded annually. What is the final value of Bill's investment at the end of year 7?

13–4. Alice Long has decided to invest $400 semiannually for 5 years in an ordinary annuity at 10%. As her financial advisor, could you calculate for Alice the total cash value of the annuity at the end of year 5?

13–5. At the beginning of each period for 5 years, Rob Flynn invests $800 semiannually at 12%. What is the cash value of this annuity due at the end of year 5?

13–6. Murphy Company borrowed money that must be repaid in 5 years. So that the loan will be repaid at end of year 5, the company invests $8,500 at end of each year at 8% interest compounded annually. What was the amount of the original loan?

13–7. Jane Frost wants to receive semiannual payments of $25,000 for 10 years. How much must she deposit at her bank today at a 10% interest rate compounded semiannually?

13–8. Jeff Associates borrowed $70,000. The company plans to set up a sinking fund that will repay the loan at the end of 20 years. Assume a 12% interest rate compounded semiannually. What must Jeff pay into the fund each period? Check your answer by table.

13–9. At the beginning of each period for 7 years, Michael Ring invested $1,200 at 10% interest compounded semiannually. What is the value of this annuity due?

13–10. Jim Green wants to receive $8,000 each year for the next 12 years. Assume an interest rate of 6% compounded annually. How much must Jim invest today?

CHAPTER 14

Self-Paced Worksheet

Cover the answers on the right and fill in each blank. After answering the question, look to the right for your answer.

Vocabulary Review

1. _____ is the process of paying back a loan (principal and interest) by equal periodic payments.
2. Cash price less down payment equals _____ _____.
3. The _____ _____ _____ is the true or effective annual interest rate charged by sellers.
4. The sum of daily balances divided by the number of days in the billing cycle equals the _____ _____ _____.
5. A _____ _____ results when money is borrowed by the holder of a credit card.
6. The total of all payments less actual loan cost equals the _____ _____.
7. The deferred payment price is the total of all monthly payments _____ down payment.
8. Open-end credit is a _____ credit account.
9. The Rule of 78 is one method to compute _____ on consumer finance loans.
10. The _____ is the finance charge a customer receives for paying off a loan early.

1.	amortization
2.	amount financed
3.	annual percentage rate
4.	average daily balance
5.	cash advance
6.	finance charge
7.	plus
8.	revolving
9.	rebates
10.	rebate

Theory Tips (and/or Cautions)

11. The finance charge can include the cost of _____ reports, mandatory bank fees, etc.
12. The formula for calculating APR is only an _____.
13. The Truth in Lending Act doesn't dictate what can be _____ for interest.
14. The loan amortization table is per _____. The table is used to calculate the monthly payment.
15. The U.S. Rule applied partial payment to interest _____ and then the remainder of the payment _____ the principal.
16. In calculating the rebate fraction, the _____ represents the sum of digits based on the number of months to go.
17. The denominator of the rebate fraction represents the sum of digits based on the _____ number of months of the loan.
18. Most companies calculate the _____ _____ as a percentage of the average daily balance.
19. A cash advance is a _____ _____ from a credit card company.
20. In calculating the average daily balance, the days of the _____ _____ has to be known to arrive at the final number of days of the current balance.

11.	credit
12.	estimate
13.	charged
14.	$1,000
15.	first; reduces
16.	numerator
17.	total
18.	finance charge
19.	cash loan
20.	billing cycle

Calculations/Applications

Do calculations on scrap paper as needed. Worked-out solutions are at the end.

21. Gail Sentner bought a new Chevrolet for $16,500, putting down $500 and paying $300 per month for 60 months. Calculate:

    a. Amount financed.
    b. Finance charge.
    c. Deferred payment price.
    d. APR by table. (Use tables in *Business Math Handbook*.)
    e. Monthly payment by formula.
    f. APR by formula to nearest hundredth percent.

22. Dan Carl is buying a new Welbilt boat for $9,500. Dan puts down $2,000 and is financing the balance at 11% for 60 months. What is his monthly payment (use the loan amortization table)?

21.	a.	$16,000
	b.	$2,000
	c.	$18,500
	d.	4.5%–4.75%
	e.	$300
	f.	4.92%
22.		$163.05

79

23. From the following, calculate the finance charge rebate and final payoff:

Loan for 12 months; $6,200; end-of-month loan is repaid: 8; monthly payment; $575

24. Paula Franc bought a desk for $900. She pays $100 a month and is charged $3\frac{1}{2}\%$ interest on the unpaid balance. What is Paula's balance outstanding at the end of month 1?

25. Calculate the average daily balance from the following (30-day biling cycle):

7/21	Billing date	Previous balance	$400
7/28	Payment		$ 40 credit
7/31	Charge		$ 60
8/6	Payment		$ 10 credit
8/13	Cash advance		$ 50

23. $89.74; $2,210.26

24. $831.50

25. $416.33

Worked-Out Solutions for Calculations/Applications Section

21. **a.** $16,500 - $500 = $16,000

b. $18,000 (60 × $300) - $16,000 = $2,000

c. $18,000 (60 × $300) + $500 = $18,500

d. $\dfrac{\$2,000}{\$16,000} \times \$100 = \$12.5$ between 4.5% and 4.75%

e. $\dfrac{\$2,000 + \$16,000}{60} = \$300$

f. $\dfrac{2 \times 12 \times \$2,000}{\$16,000 \times (60 + 1)} = 4.92\%$

22. $\dfrac{\$7,500}{\$1,000} = 7.5 \times \$21.74 = \$163.05$

23. **Step 1:**
$$12 \times \$575 = \$6,900$$
$$8 \times \$575 = \underline{4,600}$$
$$\$2,300$$

Step 2:
$$12 \times \$575 = \$6,900$$
$$\underline{-6,200}$$
$$\$700$$

Step 3: 12 - 8 = 4

Step 4: $\dfrac{10}{78}$

Step 5: $\dfrac{10}{78} \times \$700 = \$89.74$

Step 6: $2,300 - $89.74 = $2,210.26

24. $900 × 3.5% = $31.50

$100 - $31.50 = $68.50

$900 - $68.50 = $831.50

25.
7 × $400	$ 2,800
3 × $360	1,080
6 × $420	2,520
7 × $410	2,870
7 × $460	3,220
(30 - 23)	$12,490

$\dfrac{\$12,490}{30} = \$416.33$

80

Word Problem Practice Quiz

Check with your instructor for complete worked-out solutions.

14–1. Andy Troll bought a new delivery truck for $16,000. Andy put a down payment of $3,000 and paid $255 monthly for 60 months. What is the total amount financed and the total finance charge that Andy paid at the end of the 60 months?

14–2. Joan Porl read the following advertisement: Price, $17,000; down payment, $500 cash or trade; amount financed, $16,500; $399 per month for 60 months; finance charge, $7,440; and total payments $23,940.
(1) Check finance charge and (2) calculate the APR by formula to nearest hundredth percent and by table.

14–3. Barry Crate bought a desk for $7,000. Based on his income, he could only afford to pay back $900 per month. There is a charge of $2\frac{1}{2}\%$ interest on the unpaid balance. The U.S. Rule is used in the calculation. Could you calculate at the end of month 2 the balance outstanding?

14–4. Tony Jean borrowed $8,150 to travel to Europe to see his son Bill. His loan was to be paid in 48 monthly installments of $198. At the end of 11 months, Tony's daughter Joan convinced him that he should pay off the loan early. What is Tony's rebate and his payoff amount?

14–5. Jim Smith bought a new boat for $9,000. Jim put down $1,000 and financed the balance at 11% for 60 months. What is his monthly payment? Use the Loan Amortization table.

14–6. Al Rolf bought an air conditioner with $150 down and 38 equal monthly installments of $35. The total purchase price (cash price) of the air conditioner was $1,050. Al decided to pay off the bill after the 30th payment. What is Al entitled to as a rebate on the finance charge? What will Al's payoff be?

14–7. Joanne Flynn bought a new boat for $15,000. She put a $2,000 down payment on the boat. The bank's loan was for 48 months. Finance charges totaled $4,499.84. Assume Joanne decides to pay off the loan at the end of the 26th month. What rebate would she be entitled to and what is the actual payoff amount? Round monthly payment to nearest cent.

14–8. Calculate APR by table for the following advertisement:
$98.50 per month; cash price, $2,899; down payment $199, cash or trade; 36 months with bank approved credit, amount financed, $2,700; finance charge, $846; total payments, $3,546.

14–9. From the following facts, Bill Jess has requested you to caculate the average daily balance:

30-day billing cycle

3/18	Billing date	Previous balance	$880
3/24	Payment		70
3/29	Charge		350
4/5	Payment		30
4/9	Charge		400

14–10. Glen James borrowed $7,200 from Able Loan Company. The loan is to be repaid in 48 monthly installments of $199. At the end of 14 months, Glen decided to pay off the loan. What is Glen's rebate and payoff amount?

CHAPTER 15

Self-Paced Worksheet

Cover the answers on the right and fill in each blank. After answering the question, look to the right for your answer.

Vocabulary Review

1. The rate for an _____ _____ mortgage is lower than a fixed rate mortgage.
2. The _____ _____ shows how each monthly payment is broken down into interest and principal reduction.
3. A _____ mortgage is paid every two weeks rather than monthly.
4. A _____ _____ loan provides a cheap and readily accessible line of credit backed by equity in your home.
5. A _____ is a one-time payment made at closing.
6. A _____ is the cost of home less the down payment.
7. A special account set up to protect the bank is called an _____ account.
8. In a _____ _____ mortgage, the borrower pays less at the beginning of the mortgage. As years go on, the payment increases.
9. When property passes from the seller to the buyer, _____ _____ may include credit reports, recording costs, lawyer's fees, points, title search, etc.

1.	adjustable rate
2.	amortization schedule
3.	biweekly
4.	home equity
5.	point
6.	mortgage
7.	escrow
8.	graduated payment
9.	closing costs

Theory Tips (and/or Cautions)

10. In a 30-year fixed mortgage, you are locked in to the interest rate, unless you _____ to get a lower interest rate.
11. In a 15-year fixed rate mortgage you need a larger down payment. The monthly payment will be _____.
12. A graduated-payment may have _____ APR than fixed or variable rates.
13. The _____ _____ requires 26 biweekly payments a year. It shortens the term loan and saves a substantial amount of interest.
14. Home equity loans are _____ deductible.
15. Points are a _____ charge that is a percent of the mortgage.
16. A rise in _____ rates could cost a home buyer thousands of extra dollars in interest cost over the life of a mortgage.
17. In the early payments of a mortgage, most of the monthly payment goes to cover _____ with a smaller reduction in _____.
18. If you plan to own your home for a short time _____ may not be an attractive alternative to get a lower rate of interest.

10.	refinance
11.	higher
12.	higher
13.	biweekly mortgage
14.	tax
15.	one-time
16.	interest
17.	interest; principal
18.	refinancing

Calculations/Applications

Do calculations on scrap paper as needed. Worked-out solutions are provided at end.

19. Twila Griffen bought a new condominium for $110,000. She put down 10% and obtained a mortgage at 8% for 25 years. What is her (a) monthly payment, (b) the total interest cost, and (c) cost of interest for the first payment?
20. Alison Wolfe bought a new chalet for $80,000 at 9% for 30 years. Prepare an amortization schedule for the first two periods.

21. Aster Smith bought a home in Ventura, California for $110,000. He put down 20% and obtained a mortgage for 30 years at 10%. (a) What is Aster's monthly payment? (b) What is the total interest cost of the loan?
22. If in Problem #21 the rate of interest is 12%, what is the difference in interest cost?

19.	a. $764.28
	b. $130,284
	c. $660
20.	1. $600, $44 $79,956
	2. $599.67, $44.33 $79,911.67
21.	a. $772.64
	b. $190,150.40
22.	$47,836.80

82

Worked-Out Solutions to Calculations/Applications Section

19. $\dfrac{\$99,000}{\$1,000} = 99 \times \$7.72 = \$764.28$

$\begin{array}{r} 300 \times \$764.28 = \$229,284 \\ -\ 99,000 \\ \hline \$130,284 \end{array}$

$\$99,000 \times .08 \times \dfrac{1}{12} = \$660$

Note:

$12 \times 25 \text{ years} = 300 \text{ payments}$

20. $\dfrac{\$80,000}{\$1,000} = 80 \times \$8.05 = \$644$

Payment	Principal	Interest	Principal reduction	Balance of principal
1	$80,000	$600 $\left(\$80,000 \times .09 \times \dfrac{1}{12}\right)$	$44	$79,956
2	$79,956	$599.67 $\left(\$79,956 \times .09 \times \dfrac{1}{12}\right)$	$44.33	$79,911.67

21. $\dfrac{\$88,000}{\$1,000} = 88 \times \$8.78 = \$772.64$

$\begin{array}{r} 360 \times \$772.64 = \$278,150.40 \\ -\ 88,000.00 \\ \hline \$190,150.40 \end{array}$

22.

$\begin{array}{r} 88 \times \$10.29\ \ = \$905.52 \\ 360 \times \$905.52 = 325,987.20 \\ -\ 88,000.00 \\ \hline 237,987.20 \\ -190,150.40 \\ \hline \$47,836.80 \end{array}$

Word Problem Practice Quiz

Check with your instructor for complete worked-out solutions.

15–1. Jeff Jones purchased a new condominium for $129,000. The bank required a $30,000 down payment. Assume a rate of 10% on a 25-year mortgage. What is Jeff's monthly payment and total interest cost?

15–2. Bill Allen bought a home in Arlington, Texas, for $118,000. He put down 30% and obtained a mortgage for 30 years at 11%. What is Bill's monthly payment? What is the total interest cost of the loan?

15–3. Jim Smith took out a $60,000 mortgage on a ski chalet. The bank charged 3 points at closing. What did the points cost Jim in dollars?

15–4. Bill Jones bought a new split-level home for $190,000 with 20% down. He decided to use Victory Bank for his mortgage. They were offering $11\frac{3}{4}\%$ for 25-year mortgages. Could you provide Bill with an amortization schedule for the first month?

15–5. Janet Fence bought a home for $215,000 with a down payment of $50,000. The interest rate was $10\frac{1}{2}\%$ for 35 years. Calculate Janet's payment per $1,000 and her monthly mortgage payment.

15–6. Marvin Bass bought a home for $170,000 with a down payment of $20,000. His rate of interest is $11\frac{1}{2}\%$ for 25 years. Calculate Marvin's payment per $1,000 and his monthly mortgage payment.

15–7. Using Problem 15–6, calculate the total cost of interest for Marvin Bass.

15–8. Marsha Terban bought a home for $200,000 with a down payment of $40,000. Her rate of interest is 12% for 35 years. Calculate her (1) monthly payment, (2) first payment broken down into interest and principal, and (3) balance of mortgage at the end of the month.

15–9. Tom Burke bought a home in Virginia for $135,000. He puts down 20% and obtains a

83

mortgage for 25 years at $12\frac{1}{2}\%$. What is Tom's monthly payment and the total interest cost of the loan?

15–10. Susan Lake is concerned about the financing of a home. She saw a small cottage that sells for $60,000. If she puts 20% down, what will her monthly payment be at (1) 25 years, 10%; (2) 25 years, 11%; (3) 25 years, 12%; and (4) 25 years, 13%? What is the total cost of interest over the cost of the loan for each assumption?

CHAPTER 16

Self-Paced Worksheet

Cover the answers on the right and fill in each blank. After answering the question, look to the right for your answer.

Vocabulary Review

1. _____ represents the owner's investment in a sole proprietorship.
2. The _____ _____ is a financial report that lists assets, liabilities, and equity.
3. Things of value owned by a business are called _____.
4. The owner's equity of a corporation is called _____ _____.
5. _____ _____ is the amount of a corporation's earnings that the company retains in the business, not necessarily in cash form.
6. _____ _____ is a method of analyzing financial reports where each amount is compared to one total.
7. _____ _____ is a method of analyzing financial reports where each amount in this period is compared by amount and/or percent to same amount in the last period.
8. _____ _____ is equal to gross sales less sales discounts less sales returns and allowances.
9. Gross profit less operating expenses equals _____ _____.
10. _____ _____ involves analyzing each number as a percentage of a base year.
11. Current ratio is current assets divided by _____ _____.
12. _____ _____ is net sales divided by total assets.
13. _____ _____ is the relationship of one number to another.
14. Savings received by the buyer for paying for merchandise before a certain date are called _____ _____.

Theory Tips (and/or Cautions)

15. Capital does not mean _____.
16. Capital is not found in the _____ _____.
17. Current assets are consumed or converted into cash within _____ _____.
18. Companies use _____ and _____ assets in their business operation rather than for resale.
19. Land is an asset that doesn't _____.
20. Current liabilities are obligations that must be paid within _____ year.
21. Horizontal analysis needs comparative columns because we take the difference _____ periods of time.
22. The _____ _____ is a financial report that is prepared for a specific period of time.
23. The _____ _____ _____ _____ doesn't represent the selling price of goods sold by companies. It represents the cost of bringing the goods into the company.
24. Sales discounts are not the same as _____ discounts.
25. The base year in trend analysis is assumed to be _____ percent.
26. In the ACID test calculation, _____ and _____ expenses are subtracted.
27. The _____ _____ ratio analyzes if assets are being utilized efficiently.
28. Many companies compare their ratio analysis to _____ standard.

1. capital
2. balance sheet
3. assets
4. stockholders' equity
5. retained earnings
6. vertical analysis
7. horizontal analysis
8. net sales
9. net income
10. trend analysis
11. current liabilities
12. asset turnover
13. ratio analysis
14. purchase discounts

15. cash
16. stockholders' equity
17. one year
18. plant; equipment
19. depreciate
20. one
21. between
22. income statement
23. cost of merchandise sold
24. trade
25. 100
26. inventory; prepaid
27. asset turnover
28. industry

Calculations/Applications

Do calculations on scrap paper as needed. Worked-out solutions are provided at end.

29. For Moore Corporation, calculate total stockholders' equity from the following: Cash, $8,000; land, $16,000; common stock, $18,000; accounts payable, $4,000; retained earnings, $6,000.

29. $24,000

30. Complete vertical analysis (round to the nearest hundredth percent):

	1997	%	1998	%
Current assets:				
Cash	$ 15,000	A.	$ 18,000	D.
Accounts receivable	13,000	B.	5,000	E.
Merchandise inventory	42,000	C.	9,000	F.
Total current assets	$150,000		$120,000	

30.   A. 10%
B. 8.67%
C. 28%
D. 15%
E. 4.17%
F. 7.5%

31. From the following information, calculate:
a. net sales; **b.** cost of merchandise (goods) sold; **c.** gross profit from sales; **d.** net income.

Gross sales, $42,000; sales returns and allowances, $4,000; beginning inventory, $8,000; net purchases, $9,000; ending inventory, $6,200; operating expenses, $8,400.

31.   a. $38,000
b. $10,800
c. $27,200
d. $18,800

32. Prepare a trend analysis from the following, assuming a base year of 1997. Round to the nearest whole percent.

	2000	1999	1998	1997
Sales	$39,000	$65,000	$31,000	$40,000

32.   1997: 100%
1998: 78%
1999: 163%
2000: 98%

33. **Given:** Total current assets, $20,000; accounts receivable, $8,000; total current liabilities, $12,000; inventory, $6,000; net sales, $40,000; total assets, $37,000; net income $8,400.
Calculate:
a. Current ratio (to nearest hundredth).
b. Acid test (to nearest hundredth).
c. Average day's collection.
d. Profit margin on sales.

33.   a. 1.67
b. 1.17
c. 72 days
d. 21%

Worked-Out Solutions to Calculations/Applications Section

29. $18,000 + $6,000 = $24,000

30.   A. $\frac{\$15,000}{\$150,000} = 10\%$ D. $\frac{\$18,000}{\$120,000} = 15\%$

B. $\frac{\$13,000}{\$150,000} = 8.67\%$ E. $\frac{\$5,000}{\$120,000} = 4.17\%$

C. $\frac{\$42,000}{\$150,000} = 28\%$ F. $\frac{\$9,000}{\$120,000} = 7.5\%$

31.   a. $42,000 − $4,000 = $38,000
b. $8,000 + $9,000 − $6,200 = $10,800
c. $38,000 − $10,800 = $27,200
d. $27,200 − $8,400 = $18,800

32.

2000	1999	1998	1997
98%	163%	78%	100%
$\left(\frac{\$39,000}{\$40,000}\right)$	$\left(\frac{\$65,000}{\$40,000}\right)$	$\left(\frac{\$31,000}{\$40,000}\right)$	

33.   a. $\frac{\$20,000}{\$12,000} = 1.67$ b. $\frac{\$20,000 - \$6,000}{\$12,000} = 1.17$

c. $\frac{\$8,000}{\frac{\$40,000}{360}} = 72\ days$ d. $\frac{\$8,400}{\$40,000} = 21\%$

Word Problem Practice Quiz

Check with your instructor for complete worked-out solutions.

16–1. The total debt to total assets of the Jones Company was .91. The total of Jones' assets was $500,000. What is the amount of total debt to Jones Company?

16–2. Beaver Company has a current ratio of 1.88. The acid-test ratio is 1.61. The current liabilities of Beaver are $42,000. Could you calculate the dollar amount of merchandise inventory? Assume no prepaid expenses.

16–3. The asset turnover of River Company is 5.1. The total assets of River are $89,000. What are River's net sales?

16–4. Jangles Corporation has earned $79,000 after tax. The accountant calculated the return on equity as .14. What was Jangles Corporation's stockholders' equity?

16–5. In analyzing the income statement of Ryan Compay, cost of goods sold has decreased from 1996 to 1997 by 5.1%. The cost of goods sold was $15,900 in 1997. What was the cost of goods sold in 1996?

16–6. Don Williams received a memo requesting that he complete a trend analysis of the following using 1998 as the base year and rounding each percent to the nearest whole percent. Could you help Don with the request?*

	1995	1996	1997	1998
Sales	$440,000	$410,000	390,000	$400,000
Gross profit	180,000	200,000	240,000	250,000
Net income	$260,000	$210,000	$150,000	$150,000

*We assume no operating expenses.

16–7. Bill Barnes has requested that you calculate the asset turnover from the following (round answer to nearest tenth):

Gross sales	$55,000
Sales discount	$3,000
Sales returns and allowances	$2,000
Total assets	$34,000

16–8. Al Bean has requested you to calculate the cost of merchandise sold from the following: Sales, $52,000; beginning inventory, $2,800; purchases, $21,500; purchase discounts, $200; and ending inventory, $6,100.

16–9. The bookkeeper of Flynn Company has requested you to calculate the company's gross profit, based on the following: Sales, $28,100; sales returns and allowances $3,000; operating expenses, $5,100; beginning inventory, $700; net purchases, $9,000; and ending inventory, $1,200.

16–10. John's Pizza has an asset turnover of 2.8. The total assets were $80,000. What were the net sales of John's Pizza?

CHAPTER 17

Self-Paced Worksheet

Cover the answers on the right and fill in each blank. After answering the question, look to the right for your answer.

Vocabulary Review

1. Cost less accumulated depreciation equals _____ _____.

2. _____ is the process of allocating the cost of an asset (less residual value) over the asset's estimated life.

3. A table showing the amount of depreciation expense, accumulated depreciation, and book value for each period of time for a plant asset is called a _____ _____.

4. _____ value is the estimated value of a plant asset after depreciation is taken (or end of useful life).

5. _____ _____ is the amount of depreciation that has accumulated on plant and equipment assets.

6. The estimated number of years the plant asset is used is called its _____ _____.

7. _____ method of depreciation spreads an equal amount of depreciation each year over the life of the asset.

8. Sum-of-the-years'-digits and declining-balance are _____ methods of depreciation.

Theory Tips (and/or Cautions)

9. _____ _____ cannot be less than residual value.

10. _____ can be indirect tax savings for the company.

11. Companies cannot depreciate _____.

12. Companies do not take the full month's depreciation for assets bought after the _____ of the month.

13. Units-of-production method is based on _____ rather than passage of time.

14. The numerator of the fraction in the sum-of-the-years'-digits calculation represents the _____ life.

15. The denominator of the fraction in the sum-of-the-years'-digits calculation remains the _____ for each calculation.

16. In the declining-balance method, you cannot depreciate below the _____ value.

17. To calculate depreciation expense in the declining-balance method, multiply the _____ _____ of equipment at _____ of year times depreciation rate.

18. In the declining-balance method, _____ _____ was not subtracted in the calculation.

19. MACRS is how a company records depreciation for _____ purposes.

1.	book value
2.	depreciation
3.	depreciation schedule
4.	residual (salvage)
5.	accumulated depreciation
6.	useful life
7.	straight-line
8.	accelerated
9.	book value
10.	depreciation
11.	land
12.	15th
13.	usage
14.	remaining
15.	same
16.	residual
17.	book value; beginning
18.	residual value
19.	tax

Calculations/Applications

Do calculations on scrap paper as needed. Worked-out solutions are provided at end.

20. Given the following, calculate the yearly depreciation expense using the straight-line method.

    Truck, $30,000; residual value, $5,000; estimated useful life, 5 years.

21. On January 1, Lyon Co. bought a machine for $50,000 with an estimated life of 8 years. The residual value of the machine is $10,000. This machine is expected over its useful life to produce 60,000 units. This machine is expected to produce 9,000 units the first year and 16,000 in year 2. Calculate the depreciation expense for the machine in years 1 and 2.

22. Pete Smith bought a truck on January 1 for $60,000 with a residual value of $15,000. The truck has an estimated life of 5 years. Using the sum-of-the-years'-digits method, calculate the depreciation expense in years 1 and 2.

20.	$5,000 per year
21.	Year 1: $6,030 Year 2: $10,720
22.	Year 1: $15,000 Year 2: $12,000

23. If Pete in #22 bought the truck on April 5, what would the depreciation expense be in years 1 and 2?

24. If in #22 Pete used the declining-balance method at twice the straight-line rate, what would the depreciation expense be in years 1 and 2?

25. Using MACRS, what would be the first year's depreciation for a waste water sewer plant that cost $700,000?

Worked-Out Solutions to Calculations/Applications Section

20. $\dfrac{\$30,000 - \$5,000}{5 \text{ years}} = \dfrac{\$25,000}{5} = \$5,000$

21. $\dfrac{\$50,000 - \$10,000}{60,000} = \dfrac{\$40,000}{60,000} = \$.67$

Year 1: $9,000 \times \$.67 = \$6,030$
Year 2: $16,000 \times \$.67 = \$10,720$

22.
```
  $60,000
 -15,000
 ---------
  $45,000
```

Year 1: $\$45,000 \times \dfrac{5}{15} = \$15,000$

Year 2: $\$45,000 \times \dfrac{4}{15} = \$12,000$

23. Year 1: $\$15,000 \times \dfrac{9}{12} = \$11,250$

Year 2: $\$15,000 \times \dfrac{3}{12} = \$ 3,750$

$\$12,000 \times \dfrac{9}{12} = \dfrac{9,000}{\$12,750}$

24. Year 1: $\$60,000 \times .40 = \$24,000$
Year 2:
```
   $60,000
  -24,000
  ---------
   $36,000 × .40 = $14,400
```

25. $\$700,000 \times .05 = \$35,000$

Word Problem Practice Quiz

Check with your instructor for complete worked-out solutions.

17–1. Alvin Ross bought a truck for $7,000 with an estimated life of 4 years. The residual value of the truck is $1,000. Assume a straight-line method of depreciation. What will be the book value of the truck at the end of year 2? If the truck was bought on September 5, how much depreciation would be taken in year 1?

17–2. Jim Company bought a machine for $5,000 with an estimated life of 5 years. The residual value of the machine is $500. Calculate the (1) annual depreciation and (2) book value at the end of year 3. Assume straight-line depreciation.

17–3. Using Problem 17–2, calculate the first two years' depreciation assuming the units-of-production method. This machine is expected to produce 5,000 units. In year 1, it produced 2,400 units; in year 2, 2,600 units.

17–4. Assume Jim Company (Problem 17–2) used the sum-of-the-years'-digits method. How much more or less depreciation expense over the first two years would have been taken compared to straight-line depreciation?

17–5. Using Problem 17–2, calculate the first two years' depreciation assuming Jim Company used the declining-balance method at twice the straight-line rate.

17–6. Able Corporation bought a car for $6,750 with an estimated life of 7 years. The residual value of the car is $450. After 2 years, the car was sold for $5,200. What was the difference between the book value and the amount received from selling the car if Able used the straight-line method of depreciation?

17–7. If Able Corporation (Problem 17–6) used the sum-of-the-year's-digits method, what would have been the difference between the book value and the price at which the car was sold?

17–8. Jerry Jeves bought a new delivery truck for $6,800. The truck had an estimated life of 6 years and a residual value of $500. Prepare a depreciation schedule for the sum-of-the-years'-digits method.

17–9. Marika Katz, owner of Katz Ice Cream, is discussing with her accountant which method of depreciation would be best for her ice cream truck. The cost of the truck was $10,200, with an estimated life of 5 years. The residual value is $1,200. Marika wants you to prepare a depreciation schedule using the declining-balance method at twice the straight-line rate.

17–10. Morris Sullivan bought a machine for $6,900. Its estimated life is 5 years, with a $600 residual value. Using MACRS, calculate the depreciation expense per year for this machine over the first 3 years.

CHAPTER 18

Self-Paced Worksheet

Cover the answers on the right and fill in each blank. After answering the question look to the right for your answer.

Vocabulary Review

1. The last-in, first-out method (LIFO) assumes that the _____ inventory brought into the store will be the first sold.

2. The _____ _____ is an inventory method that estimates the cost of ending inventory by using a cost ratio.

3. _____ _____ is the total of all inventories divided by the number of times inventory was taken.

4. _____ _____ is a ratio that indicates how quickly inventory turns.

5. In a _____ inventory system, the inventory records are continually updated.

6. In a _____ inventory system, a physical count of inventory is taken at the end of a time period.

7. The _____ _____ method calculates the cost of ending inventory is taken by identifying each item remaining to the invoice price.

8. _____ expenses are not directly associated with a specific department or product.

9. The _____ _____ _____ uses the cost percentage to calculate the estimated cost of goods sold.

1. last

2. retail method

3. average inventory

4. inventory turnover

5. perpetual

6. periodic

7. specific identification

8. overhead

9. gross profit method

Theory Tips (and/or Cautions)

10. Companies that sell high cost items usually use the _____ _____ method of inventory valuation.

11. Companies with homogeneous products like fuels and grains may use the _____-_____ _____.

12. Cost of goods available for sale less cost of ending inventory equals _____ _____ _____ _____.

13. The cost flow assumption of FIFO or LIFO may or may not exist in the actual _____ flow of goods.

14. During inflation _____ produces a higher income than other inventory methods.

15. FIFO assumes that the first goods brought into the store are the _____ goods sold.

16. The retail method does not require that a company calculate an _____ cost for each item.

17. To use the _____ _____ method, the company must keep track of the average gross profit rate.

18. The inventory turnover at _____ is usually lower than the inventory turnover at _____.

19. A _____ inventory turnover might mean insufficient amounts of inventory resulting in stockouts.

20. The two common methods of calculating the distribution of overhead are by _____ _____ or _____ _____.

10. specific identification

11. weighted-average method

12. cost of goods sold

13. physical

14. FIFO

15. first

16. inventory

17. gross profit

18. retail; cost

19. high

20. floor space; sales volume

Calculations/Applications

Do your work on scrap paper as needed. Worked-out solutions are provided at end.

21. From the following calculate by the weighted-average method (**a**) the cost of ending inventory, and (**b**), the cost of goods sold. Ending inventory shows 18 units.

21. **a.** $66.24
    b. $139.76

		Number purchased for resale	Cost per unit	Total
January	1 inventory	12	$2	$24
March	1	9	$3	$27
April	1	20	$4	$80
November	1	15	$5	$75

22. Rework #21 using the FIFO assumption.

23. Rework #21 using the LIFO assumption.

24. Bill's Dress Shop's inventory at cost on January 1 was $32,500. Its retail value is $50,000. During the year, Bill purchased additional merchandise at a cost of $170,000 with a retail value of $366,000. The net sales at retail for the year was $345,000. Calculate Bill's inventory at cost by the retail method. Round the cost ratio to the nearest whole percent.

25. On January 1, Font Company had inventory costing $65,000 and during January had net purchases of $118,000. Over recent years, Font's gross profit has averaged 45% on sales. Given that the company has net sales of $190,000, calculate the estimated cost of ending inventory using the gross profit method.

22. a. $87
    b. $119

23. a. $42
    b. $164

24. $34,790

25. $78,500

Worked-Out Solutions to Calculations/Applications Section

21. $\$24 + \$27 + \$80 + \$75 = \dfrac{\$206}{56} = \$3.68$

   $18 \times \$3.68 = \$66.24$ cost of ending inventory
   $\$206 - \$66.24 = \$139.76$ cost of goods sold

22. $15 \times \$5 = \$75$
    $3 \times \$4 = \underline{\ \ 12}$
    $\$87$ cost of ending inventory
    $\$206 - \$87 = \$119$ cost of goods sold

23. $12 \times \$2 = \$24$
    $6 \times \$3 = \underline{\ \ 18}$
    $\$42$ cost of ending inventory
    $\$206 - \$42 = \$164$ cost of goods sold

24.

	Cost	Retail
Beginning inventory	$ 32,500	$ 50,000
Purchases	170,000	366,000
Cost of goods available for sale	$202,500	$416,000
Less net sales for the year		345,000
Ending inventory at retail		$ 71,000
Cost ratio $\dfrac{\$202,500}{\$416,000} = 49\%$		49%
Ending inventory at cost		$ 34,790

25.

	Cost	Retail
Inventory, January 1		$ 65,000
Net purchases		118,000
Cost of goods available for sale		$183,000
Less: Estimated cost of goods sold:		
Net sales at retail	$190,000	
Cost percentage (100% − 45%)	.55	
Estimated cost of goods sold		$104,500
Estimated inventory, January 31		$ 78,500

Word Problem Practice Quiz

Check with your instructor for complete worked-out solutions.

18–1. Marvin Company has a beginning inventory of 7 sets of paints at a cost of $1.75 each. During the year, the store purchased 3 at $1.80, 7 at $2.50, 5 at $2.75, and 10 at $3.00. By the end of the year, 19 sets were sold. Calculate (1) the number of paint sets in stock and (2) the cost of ending inventory under LIFO.

18–2. Calculate the cost of ending inventory under FIFO for Problem 18–1. Round to nearest cent the average cost per unit before calculating the cost of ending inventory.

18–3. Calculate the cost of ending inventory by weighted average for Problem 18–1. Round to nearest cent the average cost per unit before calculating cost of ending inventory.

18–4. Jeffrey Company allocated overhead expenses to all departments on the basis of floor space (square feet) occupied by each department. The total overhead expenses for a recent year amounted to $90,000. Department A occupied 15,000 square feet; Department B, 5,000 square feet; Department C, 9,500 square feet. What is the amount of the overhead allocated to Department C? Round ratio to nearest whole percent.

18–5. In Problem 18–4, what amount of overhead is allocated to Department A? Round ratio to nearest percent.

18–6. Moose Company has a beginning inventory at a cost of $78,000 and an ending inventory costing $86,000. Sales were $410,000. Assume Moose's markup rate is 31%. Based on the selling price what is the inventory turnover at cost? Round to nearest hundredth.

18–7. May's Dress Shop's inventory at cost on January 1 was $38,500. Its retail value is $61,000. During the year, May purchased additional merchandise at a cost of $188,000 with a retail value of $402,000. The net sales at retail for the year was $352,000. Could you calculate May's inventory at cost by the retail method? Round cost ratio to nearest whole percent.

18–8. A sneaker shop has made the following wholesale purchases of new running shoes: 15 pairs at $26, 24 pairs at $27.50, and 8 pairs at $33.00. An inventory taken last week indicates that 17 pairs are still in stock. Calculate the cost of this inventory by FIFO.

18–9. The manager of Saikes Department Store is having difficulty calculating the inventory turnover at retail. The beginning retail inventory was $88,000 and the ending retail inventory was $96,000. The store's net sales were $715,000 and the cost of goods was $492,000. Assist the manager by computing the turnover to the nearest hundredth.

18–10. Over the past five years, the gross profit rate for Jerome Corp. wsa 42%. Using the gross profit method, estimate the cost of ending inventory given the following: Beginning inventory, $7,000; net purchases, $70,000; net sales at retail, $58,000.

CHAPTER 19

Self-Paced Worksheet

Cover the answers on the right and fill in each blank. After answering the question, look to the right for your answer.

Vocabulary Review

1. _____ _____ is the value of a property that an assessor sets that is used in calculating property taxes.

   1. assessed value

2. _____ _____ is a tax on specific luxury items or nonessentials.

   2. excise tax

3. A _____ is $\frac{1}{10}$ of a cent of $\frac{1}{1,000}$ of a dollar.

   3. mill

4. _____ _____ is a tax levied on consumers for certain sales of merchandise or services by states, counties, or various local governments.

   4. sales tax

5. _____ _____ is a tax that raises revenue for school districts, cities, counties, and the like.

   5. property tax

6. Cars, home, furnishings, and jewelry are examples of _____ _____.

   6. personal property

7. Land, buildings, and so on are examples of _____ _____.

   7. real property

Theory Tips (and/or Cautions)

8. The list of items that is taxed for sales tax will _____ from state to state.

   8. vary

9. Trade discounts are subtracted from the _____ _____ before sales tax is computed.

   9. original price

10. The cost of shipping, handling, and so on are _____ subject to sales tax.

    10. not

11. Sellers also take cash discounts on the _____ _____ before adding the sales tax.

    11. base price

12. _____ _____ is often calculated as a percentage of the selling price, although the tax can be stated as a fixed amount per item sold.

    12. excise tax

13. Real property and personal property are both subject to _____ _____.

    13. property tax

14. In determining the tax rate, it should be _____ _____ to the indicated digit, even if it is less than 5.

    14. rounded up

15. To represent the number of mills as a tax rate per dollar, we divide the tax rate in decimal by _____.

    15. .001

16. In calculating property tax due, the total assessed value represents the _____.

    16. base

17. In some states, a portion of assessed value is excluded from _____ _____ for senior citizens.

    17. property tax

Calculations/Applications

Do calculations on scrap paper as needed. Worked-out solutions are provided at end.

18. John Sullivan, Jr., bought a new Apple computer for $1,900. The price included a 7% sales tax. What is (a) the sales tax and (b) the selling price before the tax?

    18. a. $124.30
        b. $1,775.70

19. In the community of Rose, the market value of a home is $150,000. The assessment rate is 40%. What is the assessed value?

    19. $60,000

20. Blooker County needs $910,000 from property tax to meet its budget. The total value of assessed property in Blooker is $141,000,000. What is the tax rate of Blooker? Round to the nearest ten thousandth. Express the rate in mills (to one tenth).

    20. 6.5 mills

21. The home of Wally Waller is assessed at $75,000. The tax rate is 13.51 mills. What is the tax on Wally's home?

    21. $1,013.25

22. Lou's warehouse has a market value of $5,000,000. The property in Lou's area is assessed at 40% of the market value. The tax rate is $142.50 per $1,000 of assessed value. What is Lou's property tax?

    22. $285,000

Worked-Out Solutions to Calculations/Applications Section

18. $\dfrac{\$1,900}{1.07} = \$1,775.70$

$\begin{array}{r} \$1,900.00 \\ -1,775.70 \\ \hline \$\ \ \ 124.30 \end{array}$

19. $\$150,000 \times .40 = \$60,000$

20. $\dfrac{\$910,000}{\$141,000,000} = .0064539 = .0065 \qquad \dfrac{.0065}{.001} = 6.5 \text{ mills}$

21. $13.51 \times .001 \times \$75,000 = \$1,013.25$

22. $\$5,000,000 \times .40 = \dfrac{\$2,000,000}{\$1,000} = \begin{array}{r} 2,000.00 \\ \times\ \$142.50 \\ \hline \$285,000.00 \end{array}$

Word Problem Practice Quiz

Check with your instructor for complete worked-out solutions.

19–1. Tom Fall bought an $80 fishing rod that is subject to a 6% sales tax and a 12% excise tax. What is the total amount Tom paid for the rod?

19–2. Don Chater bought a new computer for $2,999. This included a 7% sales tax. What is the amount of sales tax and the selling price before the tax?

19–3. Moe Blunt bought a hammer from Jan's Hardware Store for $15.88 plus tax. Jan rang up the sale and looked at her sales tax chart (use table). How much is the total of the sale?

19–4. Sheri Missan bought a ring for $8,000. She must still have to pay a 6% sales tax and an 8% excise tax. The jeweler is shipping the ring so Sheri must also pay a $30 shipping charge. What is the total purchase price of Sheri's ring?

19–5. Al's warehouse has a market value of $175,000. The property in Al's area is assessed at 45% of the market value. The tax rate is $119.20 per

$1,000 of assessed value. What is Al's property tax?

19–6. In the community of Ross, the market value of a home is $210,000. The assessment rate is 28%. What is the assessed value?

19–7. Blunt County needs $690,000 from property tax to meet its budget. The total value of assessed property in Blunt is $105,000,000. What is the tax rate of Blunt? Round to nearest hundred thousandths. Express the rate in mills.

19–8. Bill Shass pays a property tax of $3,900. In his community, the tax rate is 47 mills. What is Bill's assessed value to the nearest dollar?

19–9. The home of Bill Burton is assessed at $90,000. The tax rate is 24.60 mills. What is the tax on Bill's home?

19–10. The building of Bill's Hardware is assessed at $118,000. The tax rate is $42.50 per $1,000 of assessed value. What is the tax due?

CHAPTER 20

Self-Paced Worksheet

Cover the answers on the right and fill in each blank. After answering the question, look to the right for your answer.

Vocabulary Review

1. The person(s) designated to receive the face value of the life insurance when the insured dies is called the _____.

2. _____ _____ represents the value of an insurance policy when terminated.

3. Inexpensive life insurance that builds up no cash value is called _____ _____.

4. _____ _____ is an insurance policy that is a combination of term insurance and cash value.

5. When a life insurance policy is terminated, _____ _____ include cash value, additional extended term, and/or additional paid-up.

6. _____ is a type of fire insurance in which the insurer and insured share the risk.

7. _____ represent the amount the insured pays before the insurance company pays.

8. Insurance required by law is called _____ _____.

9. _____ _____ is an optional auto insurance that pays for damages to the auto caused by factors other than from collison (fire, vandalism).

10. The _____ is the insurance company that issues the policy.

1.	beneficiary
2.	cash value
3.	term life
4.	20-year endowment
5.	nonforfeiture values
6.	coinsurance
7.	deductibles
8.	compulsory insurance
9.	comprehensive insurance
10.	insurer

Theory Tips (and/or Cautions)

11. Term insurance has no _____ _____.

12. An insurance company will never pay more than the _____ _____ of a policy.

13. Straight life insurance provides _____ protection.

14. Universal life insurance is basically a _____ _____ insurance plan with flexible premium schedules and benefits.

15. For straight life insurance, the longer the policy is in effect, the _____ the cash value because more premiums have been paid in.

16. In nonforfeiture options, the policy holder could get cash value, reduced paid-up insurance, or _____ _____ _____.

17. Life insurance is per $1,000, while fire insurance is per _____.

18. If the insurance company cancels your fire insurance they cannot use the _____-_____ _____. The result is more of a refund to the policyholder.

19. The bottom of the fraction in the calculation for coinsurance represents the _____ required to meet coinsurance. It is calculated by rate times replacement value.

20. _____ _____ covers injury to other people's autos, trees, buildings, etc.

21. 10/20 means the insurance company will pay damages to people injured or killed by your auto up to _____ for injury to one person per accident or a total of _____ for injuries to two or more people per accident.

22. If the policyholder lowers the deductible for collision comprehensive, an additional _____ results.

23. Premiums for collision, property damage, and comprehensive are not reduced by _____ _____.

11.	cash value
12.	face value
13.	permanent
14.	whole life
15.	higher
16.	extended term insurance
17.	$100
18.	short-rate table
19.	insurance
20.	property damage
21.	$10,000; $20,000
22.	premium
23.	no fault

Calculations/Applications

Do calculations on scrap paper as needed. Worked-out solutions are provided at end.

24. Alvin Hersey, age 44, purchased a $90,000, 5-year term life insurance policy. Calculate his annual premium. After 3 years, what is his cash value?

25. Gracie Lantz, age 44, purchased a $80,000 straight life policy. Calculate her annual premium.

24.	$405; no cash value
25.	$1,224

96

26. If after 15 years Gracie (problem #25) wants to surrender her policy, what options and what amounts are available to her?

27. Calculate the total annual premium of a building that has an area rating of 1 with a building classification A. The value of the building is $90,000, with contents valued at $40,000.

28. If the insured in problem #27 cancels at the end of month 8, what is the cost of the premium and the refund?

29. If in problem #28 the insurance company cancels at the end of month 8, what is the cost of the premium and the refund?

30. Ring insures a building for $160,000 with 80% coinsurance clause. The replacement value is $400,000. Assume a loss of $90,000 from fire. What will the insurance company pay?

31. Calculate the annual premium of Phil Smool who lives in territory 5 and is a classified driver 18, has a car with age 5 and symbol 2. His state has compulsory insurance and Phil wants to add the following options:

   1. Bodily injury, 500/1000
   2. Damage to someone else's property, 25M
   3. Collision, 100 deductible
   4. Comprehensive, 300 deductible
   5. Towing

Worked-Out Solutions to Calculations/Applications Section

24. $\dfrac{\$90,000}{\$1,000} = 90 \times \$4.50 = \$405$

25. $\dfrac{\$80,000}{\$1,000} = 80 \times \$15.30 = \$1,224$

26. Cash value: $80 \times \$148 = \$11,840$
    Paid-up insurance: $80 \times \$371 = \$29,680$
    Extended term: 20 year, 165 days

27. $\dfrac{\$90,000}{\$100}$ $900 \times \$.28 = \$252$

    $\dfrac{\$40,000}{\$100}$ $400 \times \$.35 = \underline{\$140}$

    $\overline{\$392}$

28. Premium: $\$392 \times \$.74 = \$290.08$
    Refund: $\$392 \times \$.26 = \$101.92$

29. Premium: $\dfrac{8}{12} \times \$392 = \$261.33$

    Refund: $\dfrac{4}{12} \times \$392 = \$130.67$

30. $\dfrac{\$160,000}{\$320,000} = \$.50 \times \$90,000 = \$45,000$

31. **Compulsory**

Bodily	$ 80
Property	$160

Options

Bodily	$251
Property	$166
Collision	$157 (124 + 33)
Comprehensive	$ 47
Towing	$ 4
Total	$865

97

Word Problem Practice Quiz

Check with your instructor for complete worked-out solutions.

20–1. Well-known actress Margie Rale, age 44, decided to take out a limited payment life policy. She chose this since she expects her income to decline in future years. Margie decided to take out a 20-year payment life policy with a coverage amount of $70,000. Could you advise Margie of what her annual premium will be? If she decides to stop paying premiums after 10 years, what would be her cash value?

20–2. Joyce Gail has two young children and wants to take out an additional $375,000 of 5-year term insurance. Joyce is 36 years old. What will her additional annual premium be? In 4 years, what cash value would have been built up?

20–3. Roger's office building has a $430,000 value, a rating of 1, and a building classification of A. The contents in the building are valued at $125,000. Could you help Roger calculate his total annual premium?

20–4. Carol Ellen's toy store is worth $50,000 and is insured for $30,000. Assume an 80% coinsurance clause and that a fire caused $150,000 damage. What is the liability of the insurance company?

20–5. Property of Al's Garage is worth $260,000. Al has a fire insurance policy of $200,000 that contains an 80% coinsurance clause. What will the insurance company pay on a fire that causes $108,000 damage?

20–6. Pete Williams had taken out a $69,000 fire insurance policy for his new restaurant at a rate of $.77 per $100. Seven months later, Pete canceled the policy and decided to move his store to a new location. What was the cost of the premium to Pete?

20–7. Earl Miller insured his pizza shop for $200,000 for fire insurance at an annual rate per $100 of $.75. At the end of 10 months, Earl canceled the policy since his pizza shop went out of business. What was the cost of Earl's premium and his refund?

20–8. Ron Tagney insured his real estate office with a fire insurance policy for $88,000 at a cost of $.48 per $100. Eight months later, his insurance company canceled his policy, because of a failure to correct a fire hazard. What did Ron have to pay for the 8 months of coverage? Round to nearest cent.

20–9. Jim Smith, who lives in Territory 5, carries 10/20/5 compulsory liability insurance along with optional collision that has a $500 deductible. Jim was at fault in an accident that caused $3,000 damage to the other auto, and $1,200 damage to his own. Also, the courts awarded $16,000 and $8,000, respectively, to the two passengers in the other car for personal injuries. How much will the insurance company pay, and what is Jim's share of the responsibility?

20–10. Marion Sloan bought a new jeep and insured it with only compulsory insurance 10/20/5. Driving up to her ski chalet one snowy evening, Marion hit a parked van and injured the couple inside. Marion's car had damage of $6,100, and the van she struck had damage of $7,500. After a lengthy court suit, the couple struck were awarded personal injury judgments of $17,000 and $8,100, respectively. What will the insurance company pay for this accident, and what is Marion's responsibility?

CHAPTER 21

Self-Paced Worksheet

Cover the answers on the right and fill in each blank. After answering the questions, look to the right for your answer.

Vocabulary Review

1. A _____ is one who owns stock in a company.

2. A _____ is a written promise by a company that borrows money, usually with fixed-interest payments until maturity (repayment time).

3. A _____ _____ is a cash distribution of the company's profit to owners of stock.

4. An _____ _____ is fewer than 100 shares.

5. The _____-_____ _____ is the closing price per share of stock divided by earnings per share.

6. The _____ _____ _____ is the annual earnings divided by the total number of shares outstanding.

7. _____ represents the distribution of company's profit in cash or stock to owners of stock.

8. _____ _____ _____ result when dividends accumulate when a company fails to pay dividends to cumulative preferred stockholders.

9. A _____ _____ results when a bond sells for less than the face value.

10. A _____ _____ results when a bond sells for more than the face value.

11. The _____ _____ _____ represents the dollar value of one share of a mutual fund.

12. A _____ _____ _____ is a mutual fund that has no sales charge.

1.	stockholder
2.	bond
3.	cash dividend
4.	odd lot
5.	price-earning ratio
6.	earnings per share
7.	dividend
8.	dividends in arrears
9.	bond discount
10.	bond premium
11.	net asset value
12.	no load fund

Theory Tips (and/or Cautions)

13. _____ _____ _____ entitles its owners to a specific amount of dividends in a year. If not paid, these dividends in arrears accumulate.

14. _____ are allowed on the floor of the exchange.

15. _____ are traded in eights of a dollar.

16. Bonds are traded in _____ of face amount and not in dollars like stock prices.

17. The _____-_____ _____ does not have one set number. It varies depending on earnings, expectations, economic conditions, etc.

18. A zero PE means the cmopany has _____ earnings.

19. When you buy or sell stock, a _____ charge results.

20. _____ _____ do not have the cumulative feature like preferred stockholders.

21. A bond may sell at a premium if the _____ rate is more attractive than other bonds.

22. The _____ _____ on a bond may be higher than the stated interest rate if one buys the bond at a discount.

23. No matter what _____ you pay for a bond, you will receive yearly interest (face value of bond times yearly interest).

24. For stocks or bonds, _____ close is not listed in today's quotation.

25. For a load fund, the _____ _____ is the NAV plus commission.

26. A front-end load would require the payment of a commission on _____ the shares, while a back-end load will pay the commission when the shares are redeemed.

27. The NAV is the _____ quote per share value.

13.	cumulative preferred stock
14.	stockbrokers
15.	stocks
16.	percent
17.	price-earnings ratio
18.	no
19.	commission
20.	common stockholders
21.	interest
22.	current yield
23.	price
24.	yesterday's
25.	offer price
26.	purchasing
27.	closing

Calculations/Applications

Do calculations on scrap paper as needed. Worked-out solutions are provided at end.

28. Ellen Walters bought 400 shares of IBM stock at $56\frac{1}{4}$. Assume a commisson of 5% of the purchase price. What is the total cost to Ellen?

29. Froll Company earns $6 per share; today the stock is trading at $66. The company pays an annual dividend of $.85. Calculate the (a) price-earning ratio and (b) yield on the stock (to the nearest tenth percent).

30. The stock of Lyon Co. is trading at $62\frac{1}{4}$. The price-earning ratio is 18 times the earnings. Calculate the earnings per share (to the nearest cent).

31. Alice Disney bought 5 bonds of AUT Company $8\frac{1}{2}99$ at 84 and 7 bonds of QUE Company at $9\frac{3}{4}98$ at 92. Assume the commission on the bonds is $4 per bond. What was the total cost of all purchases?

32. Janice Fall bought one bond for 128. The original bond was $8\frac{1}{4}99$. Calculate the current yield to the nearest tenth percent.

33. Cumulative preferred stockholders receive $.92 per share. There are 80,000 shares. For the last 4 years, no dividends have been paid. This year $280,000 is paid out in dividends. How much dividends to preferred is still in arrears?

34. Lee Winn buys 600 shares of a mutual fund with a NAV of $16.22. This fund has a load charge of 7%. What is the offer price and what did Lee pay for her investment?

28.	$23,625
29.	a. 11
	b. 1.3%
30.	$3.46
31.	$10,688
32.	6.4%
33.	$88,000 in arrears
34.	$17.36;
	$10,416

Worked-Out Solutions to Calculations/Applications Section

28. $400 \times \$56.25 = \$22,500 \times \$1.05 = \$23,625$

29. a. $\dfrac{\$66}{\$6} = 11$ b. $\dfrac{\$.85}{\$66} = 1.3\%$

30. $\dfrac{\$62.25}{18} = \$3.46$

31. $5 \times \$840 = \$ 4,200$
$7 \times \$920 = \$ 6,440$
$\$10,640 + \$48 = \$10,688$

32. $\$1,000 \times .0825 = \$82.50$

$\dfrac{\$82.50}{\$1,280} = 6.4\%$

33. 80,000 shares $\times \$.92 = \$ 73,600$
$\times 5$
$\$368,000$
$280,000$
$\$ 88,000$

34. $\$16.22 \times .07 = \$ 1.14$
$+ 16.22$
$\$17.36$
600 shares $\times \$17.36 = \$10,416$

Word Problem Practice Quiz

Check with your instructor for complete worked-out solutions.

21–1. Norm Dorian bought 600 shares of CBS at $61\frac{1}{4}$ per share. Assume a commission of 3% of the purchase price. What is the total cost for Norm?

21–2. Assume in Problem 21–1 that Norm sells the stock for $71\frac{1}{8}$ with the same 3% commission rate. What is the bottom line for Norm?

21–3. Jim Corporation pays its cumulative preferred stockholders $2.50 per share. Jim has 40,000 shares of preferred and 80,0000 shares of common stock. In 1994, 1995, and 1996, due to slowdown in the economy, Jim paid no dividends. Now in 1997, the board of directors has decided to pay out $600,000 in dividends. How much of the $600,000 does each class of stock receive as dividends?

21–4. Roger Company earns $5.25 per share. Today the stock is trading at $61\frac{5}{8}$. The company pays an annual dividend of $1.95. Could you calculate the (1) price-earnings ratio (round to nearest whole number) and (2) the yield on the stock (to nearest tenth percent)?

21–5. The stock of VIC Corporation is trading at $70\frac{3}{4}$. The price-earnings ratio is 14 times earnings. Calculate the earnings per share for VIC Corporation to nearest cent.

21–6. Jerry Ryan bought the 6 bonds of Mort Company. $11\frac{1}{2}96$ at $91\frac{1}{2}$ and 4 bonds of Inst. System 12 S 99 for $88\frac{1}{4}$. If the commission on the bonds is $3.00 per bond, what was the total cost of all the purchases?

21–7. Sue Trenta bought 500 shares of a mutual fund with a NAV of $8.75. This fund has a load charge of 7%. What is (**a**) the offer price and (**b**) what did Sue pay for the investment?

21–8. Ron bought a bond for $88\frac{5}{8}$ of Bee Company. The original bond was $6\frac{3}{4}99$. Ron wanted to know the current yield to nearest tenth percent. Could you help Ron with the calculation?

21–9. Abby Sane decided to buy corporate bonds instead of stock. She desired to have the fixed-interest payments. She purchased 5 bonds of Meg Corporation $8\frac{7}{8}99$ at $89\frac{1}{2}$. As the stockbroker for Abby (assume you charge her a $5 commission per bond), provide her with the following: (1) the total cost of the purchase, (2) total annual interest to be received, and (3) current yield (to nearest tenth percent).

21–10. Mary Blake is considering whether to buy stocks or bonds. She has a good understanding of the pros and cons of both. The stock she is looking at is trading at $60\frac{1}{8}$, with an annual dividend of $3.65. Meanwhile, the bond is trading at $98\frac{1}{4}$ with an annual interest rate of 10%. Could you calculate for Mary her yield (tenth percent) for the stock and the bond, and make appropriate recommendations?

CHAPTER 22

Self-Paced Worksheet

Cover the answers on the right and fill in each blank. After answering the question, look to the right for your answer.

Vocabulary Review

1. A _____ _____ is a visual presentation using horizontal or vertical bars to make comparisons or to show relationships on items of similar makeup.
2. The _____ _____ is the current price divided by the base years price times 100.
3. A _____ _____ shows by table the number of times event(s) occurs.
4. The _____ is a statistical term that represents the central or midpoint of a series of numbers.
5. The _____ is a value that occurs most often in a series of numbers.
6. The _____ is an arithmetic average.
7. _____ _____ are graphical presentations that involve time elements.
8. The _____ _____ is used to find an average when values appear more than once.

Theory Tips (and/or Cautions)

9. When high or low numbers do not significantly affect a list of numbers, the _____ is a good indicator of where the center of the data occurs.
10. If high or low numbers have a significant effect on a list of numbers, the _____ may be better than the mean.
11. The _____ indicates where the center of data occurs without distorting a group of numbers with one or more extreme values.
12. The median in an odd number of values is the _____ value.
13. The median in an even number of values is the _____ of the two middle values.
14. Bar graphs can be _____ or _____.
15. _____ should be of equal size.
16. A pie chart represents 100% or _____.

Calculations/Applications

Do calculations on scrap paper as needed. Worked-out solutions are provided at end.

17. Sales at Regan Realty totaled six homes for the week. They were as follows: $175,000; $180,000; $150,000; $190,000; $160,000; $90,000. Calculate the (a) mean and (b) median.
18. Computer Village counted the number of customers entering the store for a week. The results were: 1,095; 860; 1,095; 1,111; 865; 888; 1,000. What is the mode?
19. This semester, Dawn Pisai took four 3-credit courses at El Camino College. She received A's in Accounting and Business Math and B's in Logic and Psychology. What is her cumulative grade point average (assume A = 4; B = 3) to the nearest tenth?

20. Jim's cleaners reported the following sales for the first 10 days of July:

$800 $900
$400 $600
$500 $100
$800 $200
$900 $300

Prepare a frequency distribution.

21. Irwin Publishing produced the following number of bound Business Math books during the first 5 weeks of last year:

Week	Bound books
1	5,000
2	2,000
3	3,000
4	4,000
5	1,000

Prepare a bar graph.

22. Kelly Industries reported record profits of 20%. It stated in the report that sales costs were 50% and expenses were 30%. Prepare a pie graph for Kelly.

23. Today, a new Ford Explorer costs $37,000. In 1991, the Explorer cost $18,700. What is the price relative to the nearest tenth percent?

20.

Sales	Tally
100	1
200	1
300	1
400	1
500	1
600	1
800	11
900	11

Frequency

1
1
1
1
1
1
2
2

21.

22.

23. 197.9%

Worked-Out Solutions to Calculations/Applications Section

17. a. $175,000
180,000
150,000
190,000
160,000
90,000
———
$945,000 ÷ 6 = $157,500

b. ($160,000 + $175,000) ÷ 2 = $167,500

19.
$4 \times 3 = 12$
$4 \times 3 = 12$
$3 \times 3 = 9$
$3 \times 3 = \underline{9}$
42

$\dfrac{42}{12} = 3.5$

23. $\dfrac{37,000}{18,700} = 197.9\%$

Word Problem Practice Quiz

Check with your instructor for complete worked-out solutions.

22–1. The batting averages of the North Shore Community College baseball team's starting 5 are: .333, .285, .395, .250. What is the team's mean batting average?

22–2. The following are the weights of 5 men who enrolled in a fitness class. What is the median weight of the men?

250 lbs.	185 lbs.
290 lbs.	165 lbs.
310 lbs.	

22–3. Today, a new van costs $19,500. In 1980, the van cost $12,000. What is the price relative to the nearest tenth percent?

22–4. Marsha Horton received a quality point average of 3.2 for the semester from State Community College. She received 2 A's, 2 B's, and 1 C. All of her courses were 3 credits and A = 4, B = 3, C = 2, D = 1, and F = 0. Is her grade point average correct?

22–5. Marvin Shoes rang up the following sales for the day: $25, $10, $18, $25, $10, $30, $70, $70, $90, $18, and $25. What is the mode?

22–6. Foxes Gym holds an aerobics class twice a week. The weights of the participants are:

110 lbs.	170 lbs.	150 lbs.
190 lbs.	180 lbs.	130 lbs.
160 lbs.	100 lbs.	120 lbs.
160 lbs.	130 lbs.	110 lbs.
190 lbs.	100 lbs.	130 lbs.
130 lbs.	120 lbs.	140 lbs.

Construct a frequency distribution for Foxes Gym.

22–7. Using the frequency distribution in Problem 22–6, prepare a bar graph.

22–8. Morton's General Store divides its annual sales into categories as follows:

Food	32%
Medical	49%
Services	19%

If a circle graph was prepared, how many degrees would each section be?

22–9. Students rated their professor by the following code: 4—excellent, 3—good, 2—fair, 1—poor. The following are the results of a Business Math class: 4, 3, 1, 4, 1, 3, 3, 3, 3, 3, 2, 2. What was the mean of this evaluation to nearest hundredth?

22–10. The following are dropout rates for Mr. Ryal's Accounting 1 class for the fall semester of each year:

1992	1993	1994	1995	1996	1997	1998
12%	15%	25%	16%	30%	28%	45%

Construct a line graph from this data.

Notes

Notes

Notes

Notes

Notes

Notes